The Ripple Effect:

HOW A POSITIVE ATTITUDE AND A CARING COMMUNITY HELPED SAVE MY LIFE

Steven Lewis

THE RIPPLE EFFECT:
HOW A POSITIVE ATTITUDE AND A CARING
COMMUNITY HELPED SAVE MY LIFE

iUniverse books may be ordered through booksellers or by contacting:

iUniverse LLC
1663 Liberty Drive
Bloomington, IN 47403
www.iuniverse.com
1-800-Authors (1-800-288-4677)

ISBN: 978-1-4917-3821-4 (sc)
ISBN: 978-1-4917-3822-1 (e)

Printed in the United States of America.

iUniverse rev. date: 06/24/2014

Contents

Dedication

To the remarkable spirit of Harry Charles Gelber, 1951-2014, who bravely battled a succession of multiple cancers and other serious illnesses but never stopped smiling and being gracious for all life's simple things. Harry's choice was to smile throughout his journey, even in hospice.

May Harry's spirit *ripple* throughout the Universe. When we get upset over trivial setbacks, we need to stop and think of Harry's great gift, the positive spirit that, after all, is the essence of life.

Introduction

"You got to get up every morning with a smile on your face and show the world all the love in your heart...Then people gonna treat you better...", Carole King.

"Ever wake up in the morning with good feeling and positive energy coursing through your body? It's that kind of day for me. Had a good workout, eating a healthy breakfast and getting ready for today's new challenges", Steven Lewis, pancreatic cancer patient undergoing radiation treatment, CaringBridge.org, journal entry, November 7, 2007.

It's well known that good feeling and positive energy are contagious. Whether through unconscious behavior or a deliberate decision to be upbeat and enthusiastic about life, people can inspire, motivate, stimulate and encourage others to think and act similarly. A major challenge we all face is how to generate and maintain a positive attitude even when things are not going our way. Self-help books are replete with tips and advice about how to turn up our noses at and smile through everyday setbacks that may be getting us down. Other books extol the virtues of staying upbeat even in the face of life-threatening illness. Maintaining an enthusiastic spirit and attitude is, however, much easier said than done, especially when confronting prolonged discomfort and potential mortality. Differing life circumstances for each of us discourage a "simple recipe" approach for staying upbeat under life's many stresses.

Everyone, at some point, will be faced with life-threatening trauma. Whether the trauma stems from illness, injury, automobile accidents, airplane crashes, ship disasters, terrorism, crime or acts of nature such earthquakes, hurricanes or tornados, a positive attitude can enable us to think clearly, be solution-oriented and, ultimately, prevail.

This book tells the story of how my positive thinking and attitude radiated out to my spouse, family, relatives and a wide circle of friends and acquaintances and, in turn, enabled me to stay in excellent spirit throughout extensive treatment for the most deadly form of cancer. This is not a self-help book or a book written specifically for cancer patients or those with other serious illness. Rather, it is intended to describe my own daunting journey from exceptional health to lethal sickness and back again and what I learned along the way. By writing this book, I am sharing the story of how my family and I coped with my life-threatening illness.

My cancer experience will not be exactly the same as cancer events or other devastating setbacks in your life or anyone else's. There are, however, certain key aspects of my story likely to benefit a variety of different people who have undergone similar serious illnesses or those whose family members are likewise suffering. In fact, this book really should be helpful to anyone regardless of health. Even though my journey deals largely with illness, this emphasis is just a vehicle to relate the importance of maintaining a positive attitude during life's inevitable trying times. As Hans Selye, the noted expert on life stress often said, "It's not what happens to you in life, it's how you take it."

This book is unique and different because it underscores the benefits of new technology, namely recent advances in cancer treatment and the Internet for a comprehensive medical, social and spiritual approach to healing. Use of these new technologies was instrumental in giving me hope and keeping my spirit soaring and a smile on my face throughout my arduous journey. Because I was able to maintain an excellent attitude, I could harness the true power of my entire healing community - spouse, family, relatives, friends and the health professionals at Boston's Beth Israel Deaconess Medical Center – to give me the love, support, encouragement and strength needed to navigate my rocky passage. As my positive spirit radiated inspiration throughout my healing community, the huge lift my community beamed back to me sent my spirit soaring even further. A powerful cycle of positive energy was created that not only inspired me through my cancer journey but also inspired those in my healing community to stay upbeat in confronting their own life difficulties.

I really had no plans to write this book. The book does not stake a claim for me as a health "guru" or self-help expert. My story already had a life of its own through CaringBridge. org on the Internet and word of mouth and had great positive impact on a few hundred friends and relatives. I was satisfied with giving this small gift and just contented with the thought that the worst of my illness and demanding treatment regimen likely was behind me. My wife and friends, however, strongly urged me to publicize my story. They felt my experience was so special and inspiring and my story so compelling that it should be radiated out to a much wider audience. Through their encouragement, I realized the "ripple effect" that began with my CaringBridge.org website was capable of becoming a tsunami of positive energy!

While writing this book, I came to realize I'd buried most of the scary and painful thoughts of my trying experience and whisked these thoughts away to a place where they no longer terrified me. Who wants to reflect deeply on their own potentially fragile grip on life? This, in fact, was another important reason why I had to be encouraged to write the book. Because my recall of the emotional details had been fleeting, I was unable to appreciate their likely impact on readers. For this reason, my feeling about my story had been, "So what? Lots of other people and their families go through similarly dramatic life crises. Why is my tale special enough to bother putting into a book?" While composing the book and uncovering my hidden fears, I pondered this question. The answer I found within me further stimulated my writing. So many of us experience dramatic life challenges and very few share the details with a large number of people. In my case, my family and I were able to weather a potentially very negative and debilitating state of affairs by mastering creative life forces that propelled us in a precisely opposite direction… toward highly positive physical, mental and spiritual health. Others told us that we handled our tough times with aplomb and inspired themselves and their families. For this reason, we thought bringing greater attention to our story in the form of a book might be helpful to a wide array of readers.

As this book progressed, I also came to realize that unleashing my most fearful memories and putting them on paper was especially therapeutic and that this process was vital to my full mental and spiritual recovery. Several times I became too emotional to proceed with writing. After a break, I would start again. The personal catharsis I achieved by forging ahead to finish this project was instrumental in completing the cycle from robust health to deadly illness and back again to robust health.

Steven Lewis
Delray Beach, FL
May 20, 2014

Chapter 1

I Turned Yellow and My World Changed

> *"Life is what happens while you are busy making other plans"*, John Lennon.

"You're yellow…your face, your skin and the whites of your eyes are yellow!", said my wife Karen. "Yellow?, I said, what do you mean yellow?" Karen opened her bag and pulled out a small makeup mirror and handed it to me. I moved the mirror slowly around my face and sure enough, I *was* yellow. The whites of my eyes were an abnormal orange-tinged yellow. "Why?", Karen and my son Ryan asked, as we ate at a Massachusetts Turnpike rest stop on a gorgeous summer afternoon on the way to our country home in the Berkshires. As a physiologist for over 30 years, I knew right away that the yellowness my wife and son were describing was jaundice. I was not in any pain but immediately phoned my primary care doctor in Boston who suggested hepatitis A or a gallstone as possible causes. He didn't act overly concerned but told me to get examined at my local hospital in Great Barrington as soon as possible. For the next hour of driving my wife, my son and I were very quiet.

*The westbound Charlton rest stop on the Massachusetts
Turnpike is an ordinary food court, convenience store and gas
station to most people. To me, however, it is the place where I
turned yellow from jaundice and my cancer battle began.*

We arrived at our house, dropped off Ryan and our dog,
Leeza, and went straight to the hospital emergency room. I
already knew the doctor assigned to my case. He was on duty
several months earlier when Ryan, home on leave from U.S.
Army duty in Afghanistan, visited the ER with a respiratory
illness.

Details of that night's hospital stay are blurred. After blood
was taken, the doctor reiterated the possibility I had hepatitis
or a gallstone but also said a tumor was possible. I was told
a CAT scan of my abdomen was needed to check this out.
Because it was a small country hospital, it took several hours
to locate the one CAT scan technician in town. By the time
he arrived and I drank an awful barium mixture and the scan

was completed, it was 3 AM. Shortly after, the doctor returned and said the scan did not show any obvious abnormal mass. Karen and I were extremely relieved but he then added that the resolution of the scan was limited and could not detect a small tumor. He recommended I return to Boston as soon as possible for a more definitive CAT scan. A few hours later, we were all back in the car headed for the emergency room at Beth Israel Deaconess Medical Center in Boston.

En route to Boston I phoned my doctor to let him know about last night's CAT scan results and that I was going to the Beth Israel Deaconess ER. When I described my symptoms of painless jaundice the nurse who answered said, "I'm sorry" in a tone suggesting consolation from grief. Her words and tone only served to increase my rapidly growing anxiety. In the months to come, when Karen told people about my medical condition, she would frequently hear, "I'm sorry" said in the same way. Soon I'd learn what painless jaundice meant medically.

Chapter 2

High Anxiety

"How're you doing", Karen asked me as we sat for three hours in the Beth Israel Deaconess emergency room on that quiet late summer Saturday afternoon. "Fine", I said, trying to keep Karen calm while both our nervous systems pulsated with fear about my unknown health condition. How could this be happening to me? Aside from a tonsillectomy when I was 4, I'd never been in a hospital overnight. I had never smoked, exercised all my life and ate the right foods. Rarely, if ever, did I get sick and, when I did it was always very minor. Karen and I were in disbelief.

During my work-up in the Beth Israel ER that Saturday, the doctor explained and diagrammed his theory that my jaundice likely was due to a gallstone that was blocking my bile duct. While I waited for a high resolution CAT scan to screen for a possible tumor, this theory gave me hope I instead had an easily curable illness. The thought of a possible tumor gave Karen and I the chills. My mother died of pancreatic cancer in her early 60's, but she smoked for 50 years and had many other health problems. Me, with possible pancreatic cancer...I didn't think so. Based on the ER doctor's initial guess, I comforted myself with the notion I simply had a readily treatable gallstone.

After my ER workup, I was admitted to the hospital and brought to my room. Soon after, I was examined by a team of gastrointestinal specialists. The look on their faces was grave. The head of the team looked me straight in the eye and said,

"Because you have painless jaundice, there is a 90 percent chance you have cancer." I was stunned and kept insisting that the ER doctor said what I probably had was a gallstone. Karen also wanted to question him but seeing me totally yellow and hearing the high probability of cancer put a huge lump in her throat that kept her from uttering a word. I was terrified and went into deep, deep denial. I repeatedly challenged the doctor and finally he said, "I hope I'm wrong, but based on my experience I'm 90 percent sure I'm right".

When the doctors left the room, Karen and I stared into each other's eyes. Just 24 hours earlier, we were driving to the Berkshires, ready for a glorious summer weekend and thought life was grand. Now, one day later, we grappled with the likelihood I had a most deadly form of cancer. Our minds swirled with thoughts about illness, potential mortality, family and each other. Through this emotional vertigo, we clung to the hope of the 10 percent chance my illness was something other than cancer.

Later that evening a wheelchair attendant took me down to the radiology department in the basement of the hospital. Because it was a Saturday evening in the summer, the floor was closed off and the corridor was empty. Only one dim light shone near the CAT scan room and the adjoining corridors were all pitch black. This setting would frighten even a healthy person but for me, facing a definitive moment in my life, it was a scene that nearly made me panic. Karen and I were alone for several minutes until the CAT scan technician arrived. Under the one hallway light, as I was about to lose it, she took me by the shoulders, looked me straight in the eyes and firmly said, "Steven, we've already been through so much in life, the most important thing is to be as positive as we can and, together, we'll get through this with grace." Karen's encouragement could not quell my deepest immediate fears. However, as we struggled through the next hours and days her hopeful outlook became a focal point of my emerging change.

After I was wheeled away for the scan, Karen sat nearby in a dingy waiting room. For about 30 minutes, she was totally alone in the silence of the hospital's basement staring at the wall. Karen's heart was practically beating out of her chest. She was incredibly scared but knew she had to be strong to help me get through whatever lay ahead.

The following morning, the results of the CAT scan were in. Something suspicious was lurking in my abdomen that might be a malignant tumor. An additional procedure was needed to make a definitive diagnosis. I was then scheduled for a Monday morning endoscopic biopsy.

Chapter 3

Attitude Adjustment

> *"It's easy to be happy when things are going your way. The challenge is to be happy when things are not."*, Rhoda Gelber, my mother-in-law.

I remained hospitalized on Sunday waiting for my endoscopy. Karen's words about going through whatever lay ahead with grace stayed with me. So did my yellow appearance. That Sunday, the day between my CAT scan and endoscopy, became a day of deep reflection. Karen and I struggled to come to grips with the potential threat to my life. How was I… were we… going to proceed? Even with the likelihood I had a deadly disease, I made a conscious decision to heed Karen's advice and try to turn my attitude around, not only for my own sake but for hers' as well. I knew Karen had to be strong to keep me going but realized that to make this possible, I first had to be strong for her. We both needed all the positive energy we could muster, and *it had to start from within me.* I could not depend on Karen to carry the entire burden on her own. If I radiated fearfulness and pessimism, it would be impossible for her to cope. Karen had always told me I was "the wind beneath her wings" and I knew, that especially now, she needed me to lift her up. On that day, as we emotionally fortified ourselves, Karen and I did not fully recognize the dynamic of positive energy we created. Neither were we aware how much this dynamic would ultimately inspire many others in addition to us.

Earlier, Karen and I had been through the experience of keeping each other sane while our son Ryan served in the U.S. Army in Iraq, and later in Afghanistan. Trying to stay positive when your child is in a war zone obviously is very challenging but we knew we had to rise above it…and we did! Now life was testing us anew, we recognized there was no option but to prevail and this time we had our son's help! Ryan had left the Army only months before he saw me turn yellow and his yellow ribbon that still hung in our home now took on a whole new meaning.

It could have been easier, faced with my ominous cancer threat, to simply ask why me, to fade into deep depression and to just give up. That's what I naturally felt like doing but to what end? It would have created a downward spiral of anguish, both for Karen and I, and for everyone else around us. The negative energy this could have produced in my body and mind might itself have had deadly consequences. I was not going to allow that. With all my mental power and the determination in my soul, I was going to surmount this looming obstacle.

My thoughts turned to Ryan and our daughter, Mindy, Karen's elderly parents and the rest of our relatives and friends. If I actually did have cancer, how were we going to tell them? We had no previous experience with a situation like this but instinctively realized that being positive was the only logical choice. Just hearing I had cancer would make our immediate family fearful enough. Allaying this fear with our positive attitudes seemed to us a way of maintaining their energized support and minimizing their own negative emotions. If Karen and I turned negative, we would allow our family's emotions to turn negative, drain us and limit our energy for facing what might lie ahead.

On Monday morning I had an endoscopic biopsy and our worst fear was realized…

Chapter 4

Deadly Diagnosis

That Monday morning, as I was wheeled on a gurney to the endoscopy room, I was nervous and scared. However, due to the psychological transformation I began in the previous two days, I lacked panic and was as positive as could be under the circumstances.

About one hour later, Karen entered my room on the 6th floor of the hospital. When I wasn't there, she inquired at the nurse's station. One of the GI doctors assigned to my case noticed Karen. He walked toward her and grimly said, "It's not good". He told Karen I was in recovery on the main floor. The few minutes it took her to walk to the elevator, go down six floors and get to the recovery room were excruciating. On the elevator, a woman and her teenage daughter were laughing about something. Karen kept thinking, "How can they be laughing...my husband has pancreatic cancer!"

Karen entered the recovery room and saw me lying there. She moved toward me, bent over and gently kissed my forehead. She tried hard to smile realizing I had not yet been told the endoscopy results. At that moment, the doctor who had given me the 90 percent cancer risk entered the room. Karen knew what was coming and stood there motionless but relieved that she, herself, did not have to tell me. I focused my eyes on the doctor's as he gave me the diagnosis. "You have pancreatic cancer", he said. "You turned yellow because your tumor was near your bile duct, the duct could not empty normally and this caused your jaundice". He proceeded to discuss what would happen next.

After hearing the bad news, Karen felt as if a door had been slammed in her face. Part of me was listening to the doctor but I was more concerned about Karen. The doctor was talking about the next steps needed to keep me alive and at the same time my wife was standing next to me scared stiff trying to make sense of the previous few minutes. Karen was obviously holding back a wall of emotion. Luckily, I still had drugs in me from the endoscopy that tempered the enormity of the moment.

The doctor said if surgery is possible it is the best treatment to keep pancreatic cancer from spreading and also might provide a possible cure. Because my tumor was small, he believed I was a likely candidate for surgery. The required surgery was, however, major. I probably would be hospitalized for at least a week and would need several weeks to recover. He scheduled an appointment for the surgical team to meet with Karen and I that afternoon.

The doctor also said that during the endoscopy the obstruction to my bile duct that caused me to become jaundiced was relieved and that over the next few days my yellowness would disappear. He was correct. My yellow skin and eyes gradually regained their normal color. Even though I no longer looked yellow, turning yellow had changed my world forever!

Ryan was in the waiting room when Karen left me to share the grim news. The waiting area was filled…with people working on their laptops, drinking coffee and talking quietly. Karen approached Ryan, took his hands and looked him straight in the eyes, "Your dad has pancreatic cancer", she cried and she fell hysterically into Ryan's arms. Ryan held her tightly and let her cry it out as the calm and quiet of the waiting room was completely shattered. He then put his hands on Karen's shoulders, looked *her* straight in the eyes and said "Mom, we're on a mission that starts right now. We are here to help get Dad well. There's no more time for tears!"

At that point, Karen's emotional pain became so agonizing that she said to herself, "I don't want to be me". She badly wanted out of her shocking and fearful predicament. Her only way out was to psychologically rise above herself. At that moment she put herself into an "out of body" state in which she was looking down at herself from above. This was Karen's way of minimizing her emotional distress and allowing her to lead the mission to get me well. As the leader of the mission she had to be clear-headed at all times and not allow herself to cry. Psychologists call this out of body state "dissociating". It is a way of coping with extreme fear used by victims of natural disaster, airplane and ship accidents, terrorism, kidnapping and other unthinkable situations (Ripley, A, The Unthinkable, Crown Publishers, NY, 2008). Karen actually lived in this out of body state for almost the entire year that followed. A therapist that helped Karen said her reaction was highly appropriate and evidence of her being very well adjusted.

Karen looked at Ryan as if she were in boot camp. It took a few moments for her to register what had just happened but she got it! Here is her son straight home from 4 ½ years in the military where life was a sequence of completing assigned missions. Ryan's first major mission as a civilian was to help his mother cope with all that lay ahead to keep his father alive. A few weeks before my cancer diagnosis, Karen had asked Ryan if he was ever scared when he was on a mission. He said yes, but he couldn't think of being scared because he had to focus on his assignments. Karen remembered this earlier conversation with Ryan and was able to follow his example. Her assignment was to help me get well.

In the year ahead, we all benefited from Ryan's military experience. Somehow seeing this upcoming health journey as being on a mission gave it a new perspective. As in any army mission, a sequence of steps must be taken to complete it. That's how we looked at my planned return to health. Each step - surgery, radiation and chemotherapy - required completion and then, as we all urged ourselves to believe, I would be healthy again...mission accomplished!

Even though Karen and I had to live through the trauma of Ryan's being in Iraq and Afghanistan, the silver lining of his Army service was what he brought back to us. Now we were ready to fight our own war...against pancreatic cancer!

Earlier, Karen and I had overcome many obstacles to start and raise our family. In some ways, facing up to my cancer was just one more hurdle we'd have to jump, albeit a potentially deadly one.

Chapter 5

The Lewis Family History: Overcoming Life's Obstacles

"I'm sorry to have to tell you this, Ms. Lewis, but you'll need a hysterectomy. You have adhesions in your uterus and fallopian tubes and a very bad case of pelvic inflammatory disease. There is nothing else we can do for you", said the chief of gynecology at Stanford University Medical Center. That day, in the fall of 1972, when Karen was 23 years old, started a multi-year quest of numerous infertility treatments, including several major and minor surgeries. This was in the days before remarkable modern advances such as *in vitro* fertilization, egg donors, surrogate mothers, and the like removed many barriers to pregnancy and motherhood. Karen's main goal in life was to be a mother and to be told, at 23, that she would never give birth to a child, was devastating. This barrier to starting a family was the first major obstacle in our married life. Karen and I had to keep a positive attitude and be solution oriented. In retrospect, for a young couple early in married life, staying positive and upbeat through years of infertility was extremely trying.

After agonizing each month for 8 years when we realized Karen was not getting pregnant, we finally decided it was time to adopt…

While Karen was at work on a Friday in January of 1980, she received a phone call from the social worker at our adoption agency. "Karen, what are you doing on Monday?" "I have to work", she replied. The social worker said, "How would you like to come by and pick up your child". That Monday, in the midst of a torrential downpour, we met our 4-month old baby boy. Ryan Andrew made the Lewis family three.

Karen and I both wanted two children, ideally a girl and a boy. Karen especially wished for a daughter she could develop a close relationship with. She planned to name her daughter after Minnie, her maternal grandmother. Pregnancy remained elusive, so we kept our names on the adoption list.

Two years later, Karen called Planned Parenthood for the pregnancy results from a specimen I dropped earlier that morning. "Congratulations Mrs. Lewis, it's positive", the voice at the other end of the phone said. Karen replied, "Are you sure you have the right person...my husband dropped the specimen off this morning...he was tall and thin with blue eyes." "Yes, Mrs. Lewis, we're sure!" Karen hung up stunned but still in disbelief so she called her doctor for an immediate appointment.

Upon examination, the doctor confirmed the pregnancy, put the ultrasound right on Karen's abdomen and there it was...thump, thump, thump...a heartbeat! Karen already was almost 3 months pregnant. Enter Mindy Gayle - on Karen's 33rd birthday - and now the Lewis family was four.

And so, after a very challenging start, the Lewis family was complete. In their early years together, Ryan and Mindy were inseparable buddies. However, as their pre-teen years approached, their especially close relationship began to deteriorate. Ryan, loving, compassionate and smart struggled with limited social and organizational skills, slower than average processing of information and a several eccentricities. In spite of his intellect, Ryan's shortcomings made it difficult for him to keep up in school.

In direct contrast, Mindy, was highly organized and efficient, excelled academically, creatively and athletically and was a classic, driven over-achiever. She constantly challenged

Karen and I with her precocious ways and became frustrated and resentful when her much more needy brother received the lion's share of attention. Mindy began to feel unloved by her parents and that her brother was loved much more.

All this led to our next challenge…how to keep the Lewis family, with extremely different personalities, together and functional. It was monumental. As the years passed, Mindy's resentment hardened into anger and, after she left for college, she largely avoided speaking to, or even about, her brother. Mindy also felt neglected by Karen and I and her resentment toward us lasted more than a decade. With considerable effort and assistance, Ryan managed to graduate from college but his need for organization and self-discipline were beyond what Karen and I could provide. We felt that joining the army would give Ryan the valuable training and experience he needed. Before college graduation, in 2000, Ryan committed to 4 years of army service. With this commitment, he had the option of choosing a specialty. He picked computers and telecommunication. In late 2003, when Ryan was a 24 year-old-soldier, we learned he had Asperger's syndrome, a neurological condition characterized by impairments in subtle communication skills, social interactions, information processing and executive functioning. Approximately one in every 250 people – more than a million Americans - have Asperger's syndrome.

On our family vacation in Hot Springs, AR, 1987.

Through all the issues Ryan and Mindy presented us with, Karen and I - though sometimes at wits end - always viewed their problems as solvable. In other words, in spite of many trying years as parents, we always stayed upbeat and committed to a positive resolution of each child's difficulties. For Karen and I, the revelation that Ryan had Asperger's syndrome and learning the specifics of this disorder was a major breakthrough. It gave explanation to years of mystery, confusion and doubt about Ryan's struggles to cope. These revelations profoundly improved our family dynamic. Ryan, who for many years felt different from most people, now clearly understood he was not lazy or incapable.

In summer 2003, Ryan's was stationed in Heidelberg, Germany and his Asperger's syndrome remained undiscovered. Shortly before Karen and I planned a visit, Ryan called us with the news he was being sent "down range". "Where's down range? Karen asked and Ryan replied, "Mom, down range means Iraq". As parents who, prior to 9/11, urged Ryan to enlist to gain necessary life and job skills, this call overwhelmed us with fear for our son's survival. Staying upbeat while coping with this became a juggling act between the three of us. To keep Karen and I from worrying, Ryan initially told us he was working on computers and remaining on his heavily fortified base on the grounds of one of Saddam Hussein's palaces outside Baghdad. Soon after, he sent a photo of himself near a large building. When I searched the Internet I learned the building my son stood in front of was Coalition Provisional Authority headquarters in the "Green Zone" in the center of Baghdad. One of his regular missions, Ryan would later confide to me, was part of a 2-man team escorting visitors to the Baghdad airport. Like many with Asperger's syndrome, Ryan had weak driving skills and, to handle threats to his Humvee, was therefore designated to be the shooter. To help all of us stay positive during his high-risk assignment, Ryan and I decided to keep this mission "top secret" from his mother.

Ryan in Saddam Hussein's chair at one of his palaces.

Ryan's return home from Iraq in February, 2004 had Karen and I breathing easier…for a while. A year later he was assigned to Bagram Air base in Afghanistan for 12 months. By this time we were "veteran parents" of a soldier. Karen and I knew we had to live life as normally as possible. We pretended our son was in the next town, read his occasional e-mails and lived with uncertainty. We resigned ourselves to accept all this, not to let it get to us and just stay upbeat.

Ryan in Afghanistan.

During Ryan's military service, Mindy graduated from college, moved to Manhattan and became a designer of men's and women's fashion accessories. After Ryan's discharge, he temporarily moved home with Karen and I and was present during all phases of my cancer journey. The positive attitudes Karen and I were able to sustain throughout my journey set a good example for both Mindy and Ryan and were a source of inspiration for them. If Karen and I were not positive it would have been much more difficult for our kids to cope.

With Karen and I in Massachusetts and Mindy in New York, we were concerned about her hearing my cancer diagnosis over the telephone while she was alone. We decided to notify Jon, Mindy's boyfriend of more than 2 years and have him tell Mindy I had pancreatic cancer. In Mindy's words, "Jon came over after work and I knew something was wrong. I remember telling him that he looked sad…like a boy who had lost his dog. He sat there, looking like he had something to get off his chest. All I could think was that he was going to break up with me. Then something far worse happened…words came out of his mouth that I never thought I would hear. "Your mother called me today…your father has pancreatic cancer."

"After the initial shock and tears, I called my parents. As they explained the location of the tumor was favorable, thoughts raced through my head…guilty thoughts. Was this somehow my fault?"

"Growing up, I was not an easy child…to say the least. My father's temper was put to the test on numerous occasions. At times, my parents felt as if I shut them out of my life completely…as if I wanted nothing to do with our family. I know this caused them a great deal of pain, but I continued to "build my wall" and block them out. After learning the news about my father's cancer, I tried to go to sleep…but sleep was the last thing I could do. Why was I so selfish over the past 25 years? If he doesn't beat the cancer, am I the one responsible for all the stress my family experienced?"

"After my father became ill, I would call my parents and both of them had such strength in their voices…as if nothing was wrong. The option of "if he doesn't make it" didn't exist. Rather, "when he beats the cancer" prefaced all of their sentences. "When he beats the cancer, your father is going to go back to work." "When he beats the cancer, your father will one day walk you down the aisle at your wedding." The more I listened to my parents, the more I began believing that there really was only one option…he would beat the cancer."

"Now, my father is healthy. I am relieved but in my mind that was the only possible outcome. My father is a survivor. And for that matter, my mother, brother and I also are survivors. We are all survivors for never once believing that the cancer would beat my father and that the only option was my father would beat the cancer."

Ryan's feelings about my illness were that, "As the initial months passed, I felt vulnerable and scared. Dad always helped and protected me from things I did not fully understand. Now he needed my help. I felt scared because he never needed this kind of love before to face such a problem. I would have to be his rock. And Mom's too."

"Dad's illness taught me some very important emotional lessons. Dad helped me learn to never doubt myself in what I can achieve. I think he taught everyone that by surviving with such grace. Dad is a very special person to me and I know he will overcome whatever obstacles are in his path."

Chapter 6

Drawing Up Our Battle Plan

The day after my cancer diagnosis, Karen, Ryan and I began planning our mission to restore me to good health. We realized the coming year would be arduous for all of us but knew that surrender was not an option. We understood our success depended on teamwork and that included keeping each other in the best of spirits at all times. Also, we were determined to, as best we could, keep our lives as normal as possible. Laughter and humor always had been a major part of our family's spirit and we intended to continue this.

Later that day, Dr. Mark Callery and his surgical team entered the room and introduced themselves. They proceeded to tell me about the surgery I would be having called the Whipple procedure. In this surgery, they would open my abdomen and take out the portion of my pancreas that contained the tumor. I would also lose my gall bladder, one of my bile ducts and a piece of my small intestine. My stomach would remain intact but its position would change. For someone who lived in Boston for 17 years, this sounded a lot like our "Big Dig", the recently completed multi-billion dollar project that dramatically altered the Hub's downtown traffic flow. By analogy, Dr. Callery said that the Whipple surgery would redirect my flow of digestion. He showed me some pictures of the digestive system before and after the procedure and referred me to a website for more details.

Because of my physiology background, the surgical process made sense to me. Personally, however, I was concerned because in my 59 years of life I'd become very attached to my digestive system. Together, my digestive system and I had enjoyed many a fine meal and savored many tasty libations. Even though we knew we were in for some changes post-operatively, my digestive system and I were ready to make any necessary sacrifices to eat, drink and be merry again.

I was greatly comforted by Dr. Callery's renowned surgical skills and the fact that he and his team regularly performed several Whipple procedures each week. His beside manner also was quite reassuring. When Karen was introduced, Dr. Callery warmly said, "So this is your beautiful bride". The "beautiful bride" sobriquet stuck and I began to use it when referring to Karen. Later on, Dr. Callery would tell us he also calls his wife, "my beautiful bride". Naturally, Karen took a quick liking to Dr. Callery. She bonded with my surgeon as her husband's savior, the man who would return him to good health. Karen hugged Dr. Callery tightly that day and every time they met thereafter.

Dr. Callery said I was lucky my tumor was near my bile duct and that I turned yellow from jaundice. Most pancreatic tumors begin in a different location and have already grown very large and spread before the patient is diagnosed. By then, surgical removal of the tumor is either impossible or unlikely to be curative. This is why pancreatic cancer has had such a low survival rate.

He told me my tumor was small. If he could extract it all no further treatment might be needed and I could be considered cured. He could not, however, guarantee this best possible outcome. In spite of this, Karen and I had high hopes for a cure and also that I'd heal rapidly and be back to work in 30 days.

We decided to schedule my surgery as soon as possible… on the following Tuesday morning, August 28th. This gave

Karen and I a week to search our souls, plan communication to family and friends about my illness and prepare for the surgery and what might lie beyond.

An aerial view of our Berkshire home.

It was most conducive to my spirit to spend the week prior to surgery in nature at our Berkshire country home. The Berkshires is a special place for Karen and me. We have many delightful friends and neighbors with whom we've "smelled the roses" and enjoyed life. Our plan was to socialize as much as we could in the week prior to my surgery. In that remarkable week, I gained an incredible new perspective on how I could get through my illness while minimizing my psychological stress.

Chapter 7

Paranormal

During the week before my surgery, Karen and I shared my cancer diagnosis and upcoming surgery with Berkshire friends and neighbors. For me, a very private person, this was a major change. I was heartened to learn that one neighbor, a generally well and physically active man about my age, was in the process of beating thyroid cancer. His spirit was incredible and he exuded tremendous confidence that cancer was beatable if you were generally a healthy and physically fit person. To me, a "rookie" in the cancer game, this helped tremendously to alleviate my fear and give me hope. This man was the first friend I allowed into the inner core of my cancer journey. He and his wife also gifted us by suggesting we start a CaringBridge.org (see Chapter 8) website to communicate my story and progress to our relatives and friends. As soon as they explained the benefits of CaringBridge.org and how easily well-wishers could send messages of encouragement, a light went on in my mind. I immediately realized what a powerful tool this would be for Karen and me to send and receive positive healing energy and ease our communications burden.

On the very same day, I also discovered that, in addition to my friend who was presently battling thyroid cancer, our other nearby neighbor miraculously survived a few years earlier when his heart stopped 3 times in one day. Both neighbors were men about my age who remained well and very physically fit. Opening my feelings to both neighbors provided me a vital lesson. Only after I shared my cancer diagnosis did they relate their uplifting stories and advice about surviving life-threatening illness.

One neighbor in fact told me that very few people were privy to the details of the health crisis he had shared with me. Naturally, I was honored and the positive value of sharing my own health condition was reinforced.

I found that opening up and sharing the details of my story – while, of course, remaining in positive spirit – made others feel positive and comfortable with sharing information uplifting to me. As the week of preparation for my surgery progressed, I put this into practice with all friends Karen and I socialized with. My outpouring of positive led to a growing surge of positive energy beamed back to me as my day of surgery approached. Moreover – and I say this with reservation because of my scientific background – later on the day that I spoke with both my neighbors, I actually had a miraculous paranormal experience that symbolically augured the successful navigation of my cancer journey.

That afternoon as I walked slouching toward my bedroom and approached the open bedroom door with my mind on nothing in particular, I felt multiple bolts of energy on both sides of me that jolted me under both arms and snapped my walking posture to the most erect position. The energy, which lasted a few seconds, came from the directions of my neighbors' homes. The sensation was like nothing else I've ever felt. I was astonished by the flow of positive energy it created within me.

I interpreted this paranormal experience as a spiritual gesture from both these survivors of life-threatening illness that would serve as positive inspiration for my coming trials of surgery and whatever lay beyond. This momentous experience was life-altering and unforgettable. As a scientist for more than 30 years, I had never believed in anything but black and white proven facts and was highly skeptical of paranormal phenomena. Now, here I was, struck by uplifting forces that were solid reality to me but obviously unexplainable by normal science. I rushed to tell Karen what had occurred and she looked at me as if I was crazy. Until then, she knew me well as someone who had no tolerance for anything but the facts. Here I was telling her that "force fields" had hit me and lifted me up. Karen had been numb dealing with thoughts of my cancer diagnosis and upcoming surgery. Even though she herself believed it was possible to have a paranormal experience, she was amazed that I actually had one and that I accepted it as truth. As our week in the Berkshires progressed and Karen and I had many deep conversations about life, we began to believe that my paranormal was the "Universe" telling us to have faith that all would be okay.

Chapter 8

CaringBridge.org:
My Healing Community on the
Information Superhighway

> *"The first request Dad makes when we enter his (hospital) room in the morning is: "read me the new messages!"*...Ryan Lewis, CaringBridge.org journal entry, August 30, 2007.

CaringBridge.org, a website that enables seriously ill patients to create blogs about their progress, greatly eased my cancer journey. The first entry, called "My Story", posted two days before surgery, included the events leading up to my cancer diagnosis and plans for my surgery and recovery. Within a day, I had ten incredibly supportive guest messages from friends and relatives. My first CaringBridge.org journal update was posted the next day, less than 24 hours prior to surgery. The following morning, before I left for the hospital, I woke up early and found twenty-five new guest messages. The total of thirty five messages received before my surgery were spiritual inertia for the current of positive energy begun by Karen and me during my tests and diagnosis and my jolting paranormal experience.

At least once a week I'd post updates on my treatment progress and how I was feeling. In response, almost every day my CaringBridge.org website contained several new messages of love and encouragement from relatives and friends. The messages I received were heartfelt emotional outpourings that took real effort to compose and kept my "spiritual tank" topped off (see Appendix for samples of my CaringBridge.org guest messages).

A phone call or store-bought get-well card with a sentence or two and a signature cannot be compared to CaringBridge. org. Had my cancer ordeal happened before wide-spread use of the Internet, I likely would have received phone calls at awkward times and greeting cards that were much less personal than a CaringBridge guest message composed from scratch. Also, Karen would never have been able to cope with disseminating my progress to the more than 100 people who regularly visited my CaringBridge.org blog. Back and forth communication with my caring community by phone would have been repetitive and awkward and would have exhausted Karen physically and emotionally.

Each morning of my cancer journey, reading my messages was the first thing I looked forward to and I couldn't wait to share them with Karen. Also, I tried to make my journal entries as positive and humorous as possible because I realized this was the best way to receive upbeat responses. Just as I knew I had to be strong for Karen so she could be strong for me, I realized I could not depend on the many regular readers of my blog to continue to send uplifting messages if the tone of my entries centered on complaint. Everyone struggles with big and small life problems of their own. If I repeatedly complained, I would have worn down the good intentions of friends and relatives. Regularly planning my next positive and humorous CaringBridge.org update also was a great way to keep from dwelling on my discomfort and fatigue.

As my months of treatment continued and the volume of my CaringBridge.org journal entries, website visits and guest messages snowballed, so did my confidence for a successful outcome of my cancer journey. My increased confidence reflected the cycle of positive energy that the CaringBridge. org process helped create. With my website, I possessed a growing historical record of my thoughts and feelings and the guest responses at each stage of my illness. Because all guests could access this material and see the messages others wrote, a spiritual community of healing was created. In response to almost 100 journal entries I made, I had nearly 10,000 visits to my CaringBridge.org site and more than 1,000 guest messages were received from over 100 families, groups and individuals. This was – and still is – tremendously uplifting to my spirit.

In order to derive maximum benefit from CaringBridge. org, I had to be comfortable with opening up and sharing my cancer journey with whomever read my website. For me, normally a very private person, this was a sudden metamorphosis. In order to embrace this level of openness, I first had to get through the stage of denial that typically occurs soon after cancer is diagnosed. During the week between my diagnosis and surgery, I rapidly began to accept the reality I had cancer. Talking with neighbors who had life threatening illnesses and socializing with other close friends, helped me compress my denial stage. The more I discussed my cancer with those around me the better I felt. It seemed as if talking about my illness helped melt away my anxiety over its potentially fatal outcome. As this occurred, I actually looked forward to starting my website only six days after I was diagnosed.

Use of a CaringBridge.org healing community based on Internet technology exemplifies a modern approach to dealing with cancer. Openness is a key factor. This openness of posting details of my cancer journey for all to read on the Internet contrasts starkly with my parents' generation in which cancer diagnosis and treatment was often barely discussed even among family members. This is because 20 to 30 years ago a cancer diagnosis was typically a death sentence and many thought superstitiously that if you didn't talk about it, it might disappear. In her book, *The Human Side of Cancer*, (Harper, New York, 1999) Dr. Jimmie Holland, a psycho-oncologist at Memorial Sloan-Kettering Cancer Center, notes that until the 1970s, the word cancer rarely was mentioned to patients. Medical schools taught that giving the diagnosis directly to a patient would take away all their hope. As an example of how the oldest generation still thinks about cancer, when we called Karen's parents, 91 and 86 years old, to share my diagnosis, Karen's mother burst into tears and said, "It should be me, not him, I'm older". My mother-in-law cried every day for several months. To my in-laws, who'd seen many close friends and relatives die of cancer, hearing my diagnosis was tantamount to my death.

In the past decade, tremendous advances in cancer diagnosis and treatment to some extent have tempered people's fears. The fact that cancer is no longer considered a definite death sentence but in many cases is a treatable and possibly curable disease has softened attitudes and increased people's willingness to share information. Today, on the Internet, there are many websites chock-full of accurate medical information about a variety of different cancers and numerous sites and Facebook groups where cancer patients can share their stories. The fact is that in their lifetimes, one out of every two men and one out of every three women will receive a cancer diagnosis. People want to learn how others cope with cancer, to perhaps make it easier for themselves or friends or relatives who have been or may be stricken. For me, one benefit of sharing my cancer story is that I heard many instances of people who had beaten incredible odds to survive cancer and other life threatening conditions. Hearing these stories gave me tremendous hope.

Sharing information about cancer through venues should CaringBridge.org and Facebook can radiate great hope and inspiration to a large audience. Many healthy friends who left guest messages, indicated how much my website inspired them. For example, one friend who would typically moan and complain about difficulties with business deals would check my website, realize how lucky he was to be in good health and quickly return to a positive state of mind. A colleague of Karen's would check my website each morning before work and start each day energized by the knowledge her husband was healthy and not creating a drain on her (other examples are in the Appendix). A main reason why my own CaringBridge. org website inspired such hope is that only about 5 percent of pancreatic cancer patients survive and most die within a few months. In contrast, here I was feeling pretty good, keeping positive and cracking jokes on my website as my cancer journey moved forward.

Chapter 9

The Big Dig in My Abdomen and the Smile That Wasn't There

On the morning of my surgery, Karen awoke early and puttered in the kitchen trying to act as if it were a normal day. Ryan was soundly asleep and Karen did not want to wake him because she wanted the pre-surgery time alone with me. During our ride to the hospital we both were silent. The surgical waiting room was noisy, crowded and lacked sufficient seating. It was not conducive to quiet contemplation or conversation before a major operation. I was frightened but determined to be upbeat. I summoned all my positive energy – from Karen, from my paranormal experience of the previous week and from all our friends and relatives who spoke to us and left messages on my website.

Along with the positive attitude that helped Karen and I psychologically, a key factor was the hope for a cure. The Whipple surgery was the treatment of choice for a cure and the best outcome was for the entire pancreatic tumor to be removed. If the cancer had not spread and the tumor was completely cut away, I might be considered cured and no further treatment would be needed. If any cancer remained, radiation and chemotherapy would be required. Naturally, going into surgery, Karen and I had tremendous hope the tumor would be totally excised and I would be back to work after 30 days of recuperation. The pathology report on my pancreatic tissue would be complete about one week after surgery. Our vision was that Dr. Callery would present us with the surgical result by walking into my room with a big smile on his face and saying, "We got it, you're cured!" In the meantime, surgery and first week of recovery presented the most immediate challenge.

My upbeat attitude continued in the pre-op room. Just before I laid down on the gurney that would wheel me into surgery, I gave the assistant surgeon the "thumbs up" sign… with both thumbs! He smirked. Did he think I was cool, crazy or just plain stupid, knowing what was about to happen and how my body would be changed forever? The way I looked at it, my true goal was to live and be well and there really was no alternative to thinking and acting positive. So, whatever the surgeon thought, my feeling was, "Bring it on…get this cancer gone!"

As I was wheeled toward the operating room, Dr. Callery hugged Karen before she left. My wife and my surgeon looked at each other without exchanging words. Dr. Callery's expression was upbeat, a "see you later, I've got work to do" appearance.

While I was on the operating table, Karen drove home in a trance-like state. She pulled into the driveway and sat quietly in the car for a few minutes. She then went upstairs to wake Ryan and tell him I was in surgery. As Karen busied herself during that day, she worried about me but was buoyed by the fact that my attitude was great, my surgeon was experienced and confident and my hospital had an excellent reputation.

Nowadays, the Whipple surgery typically takes about 7 hours to complete and the procedure itself is much more complex than a heart transplant. The Whipple procedure had its origins in the 1930's and, as recently as the 1970's, it could take about 15 hours and 25% of the patients died from the surgery itself. By the year 2000 only 5% died. However, in the hands of Dr. Callery's experienced team, the mortality rate was much lower. Recovery from this extensive surgery was another issue. One man I knew who had the Whipple 30 years earlier spent three months recovering in the hospital. Fortunately, my post-surgery hospital stay was expected to be about 8 to 10 days. For me, 10 days in the hospital was 10 days too long. Thankfully, I really didn't know what was in store for me.

If you don't know human anatomy, but are familiar with New York geography, it's easy to visualize what Dr. Callery and his team did to my pancreas in the Whipple surgery.

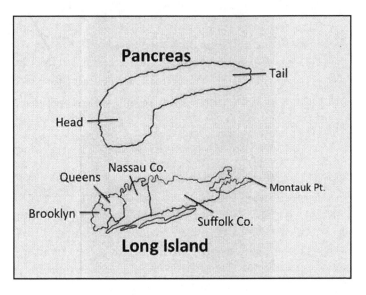

New York's Long Island runs east-west (i.e. close to horizontally) with its eastern tip, at Montauk Point, slightly more north than its western side which consists of the New York City boroughs, Brooklyn and Queens. Likewise, in healthy people, the pancreas runs close to horizontally in the human abdomen from the pancreatic tail to the pancreatic head. The tail of the pancreas, analogous to Long Island's Montauk point, is located slightly higher than the head of the pancreas, analogous to Brooklyn and Queens. My tumor was located in the head of my pancreas; that is, approximately "in Brooklyn". During the Whipple surgery, Dr. Callery removed the tumor by excising about one-third of my pancreas on the side of the pancreatic head. This roughly corresponds to slicing Brooklyn and Queens off Long Island and leaving Nassau and Suffolk counties. My wife, Karen, who grew up in Nassau County, always was frustrated she couldn't get all the "Brooklyn" out of my persona. At least now she could say the "Brooklyn" was no longer in my pancreas.

Regaining consciousness after the Whipple surgery was probably the scariest experience of my life. For the first 10 seconds I couldn't see and I couldn't breathe; it was like awakening in hell! Luckily, these two problems soon got resolved. The next issue was dealing with myself as a Rube Goldberg-like contraption featuring tubes in my nose, in the arteries and veins of my wrists and in the large vein leading to my heart, as well as an assortment of bandages covering sutures and staples over a wide swath of my middle.

"What took you so long?" I said when Karen entered the recovery room. In spite of my medically grotesque appearance, I was upbeat and smiling and the tension of Karen's day-long wait melted away. For both of us, the recovery process had now begun.

To protect my delicately rearranged digestive system, I was not allowed to eat or drink for the first two days post-operatively. Then, for the next couple days, I was allowed a shot glass of water every few hours. My daughter joked that one "shot" every few hours is not my usual rate of consumption of liquids served in a shot glass. While my digestive system rested, my veins took up the slack. Together, my veins and I enjoyed four days of scrumptious I.V. meals. Food preparation was energy efficient and easy…no ovens, gas ranges or microwaves were needed. The nurse just hung the I.V. bag, connected the tube and adjusted the drip. The first real food I tasted – a small cup of chocolate ice cream - was almost 5 days after surgery. It was the most glorious meal I ever consumed.

The doctors and nurses told me I was a poster child for the Whipple operation. They rarely saw anyone recuperate so well and with such a great attitude. As often as strength would allow, my I.V. pole and I surged forward for long walks through all corridors. With my exercise program and no solid food, I was a dieters dream. Pounds just melted away - about 20 of them during my hospital stay. A chart on my wall listed all the checkpoints I'd have to meet for an on-schedule, 8 to 10 day recovery from the Whipple procedure. I hustled along, stayed ahead in my progress and completed recovery in just 7 days.

As a hospital patient, a good night's sleep is almost impossible. I was awakened repeatedly for injections, blood draws and a host of other procedures such as blood pressure and temperature measurements. After a few days, I felt like a pincushion from getting stuck so often. As my week in the hospital finished, I badly wanted out. The surgery, hospitalization and starting all over with a new digestive system still had me in complete disarray.

On my last day in the hospital, Karen, Ryan and I were sitting in the sunny patient lounge waiting for my pathology report. After a while, Dr. Callery appeared but the smile we had envisioned was not there. "I have good news and I have bad news", he said. "The first good news is that I removed more than 99% of the tumor. Other good news is that there was no evidence of cancer activity in the lymph glands I removed. The bad news is that the pathology report showed a few remaining cancer cells that I couldn't see during the surgery. These cancer cells were in an area of the pancreas bordering your portal vein, the vein that carries nutrients to your liver. This is too delicate an area to operate on." Naturally, I was greatly disappointed to hear that after undergoing this grueling surgery, I still had cancer in my pancreas but I was willing to accept Dr. Callery's explanation. Karen instead was much more worried. She pressed Dr. Callery for a percentage chance I would be live and be well. Because there is so much variation from patient to patient in how they tolerate and respond to the Whipple surgery and treatment, Dr. Callery was reluctant to give Karen a percentage chance. When she pushed him further, he finally said that overall, of patients with a few cancer cells remaining after the Whipple, about 40 percent will survive more than 5 years. Hearing this made Karen extremely fearful and over the next days and weeks she would scour the Internet for any and all information that might help us out of this predicament. Before he left, Dr. Callery said I might be a good candidate for CyberKnife radiation therapy, a new high-tech tool for cancer fighting. He set an appointment for me with Dr. Anand Mahadevan, the specialist in Beth Israel's radiology department who did cutting-edge research on CyberKnife technology for killing pancreatic cancer cells.

Chapter 10

My Return Home and
Surprise Birthday Party

> *"Your full-time job is to get better",* Dr. Anand
> Mahadevan, Beth Israel Deaconess Medical
> Center.

Recuperation from the Whipple procedure took about a
month.

On September 4th, a week after Whipple surgery, I was
back home with a new road map for my digestive system. Being
home was exhilarating – sunny skies, fresh September air, no
more IVs or being woken up every few hours for injections. It
was time to work on "the care and feeding of me". Initially,
my care and feeding mostly consisted of sleep, an occasional
walk down the driveway, to the mailbox or around the block,
and bland tasteless food.

I didn't have GPS inside my abdomen, so my digestive
system and I had to learn to navigate using our own intuitions.
At the beginning, it was a case of the blind leading the blind.
There were many unknowns and lots of post-surgery digestive
awkwardness. How much of this was due to missing a portion
of my pancreas, to my new digestive roadmap itself, to
incomplete healing from the surgery and/or to the medications
I was taking? It was difficult to sort all this out, so naturally,
my digestive system and I stumbled around quite a bit. Some
days it was like we were participating together in a 3-legged
race and a limbo contest at the same time.

There also were psychological sacrifices my digestive system and I had to make. For someone who loves Indian and Mexican food and an occasional margarita, my early post-surgery diet of cream of wheat and plain boiled chicken and fish washed down with tea was a hardship cuisine. My digestive system and I knew we would not be content until we could eat the things we loved. Also, eating in general wasn't fun for a couple months. After my surgery, foods tasted much blander than I'd remembered. As time passed and I returned to Mexican and Indian restaurants, I would order the spiciest dishes on the menu. It seemed that only these spicy items could counteract the tendency for most food to taste bland. Through all these adjustments, it seemed as if my digestive system and I took turns playing shrink and patient.

Following a post-surgery check-up, Karen and I arrived in the Berkshires with plans for an extended recuperation before my first therapy, Cyberknife radiation, in early October. September weather in the Berkshires often is spectacular. Most days are sunny, warm and breezy and the evenings are cool and great for sleeping. As September rolls on, the deciduous trees start to turn their remarkably beautiful fall colors. The therapeutic feeling of all this nature did wonders for my body and soul. What a great start to my recovery!

For my birthday in mid-September, Karen and I and another couple planned to visit a friend's home for a quiet dinner. I still ate gingerly, tired easily and slept a lot. In spite of this, I looked forward to celebrating my birthday on a quiet evening with close friends. Still a bit groggy from a late afternoon nap, I was totally unprepared for the greeting of a crowd of about 70 friends yelling, "Surprise!" How many people have a huge surprise birthday party 2 ½ weeks after a Whipple surgery?

It was a very emotional moment for me. Less than a month before, I'd been diagnosed with a particularly lethal form of cancer. Less than two weeks before I'd left the hospital after 7 hours of major abdominal surgery. My digestive system and I were struggling to understand and cope with a new roadmap. I was taking 25 pills per day and sleeping a lot. Life was definitely different now, but it also was my 59th birthday and through my medicated state, as the guest of honor, I was determined to participate and enjoy.

Within minutes I had another surprise…my daughter and her boyfriend had arrived from New York to share in the celebration. My whole family and all my friends now surrounded me on my big day. Karen, Ryan and Mindy gave a speech in my honor. Their words touched me so. The power of love and deep concern for me and the positive energy of the crowd in that room was simply overwhelming.

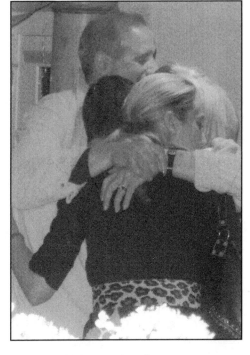

*Karen, Mindy, Ryan and me hugging at my surprise
birthday party after my Whipple surgery.*

In the Lewis family, we frequently have used the phrase, "Go For It" to encourage vigorous pursuit of an important goal by one or more family members. The "Go For It" phrase is often inscribed on family pictures and cakes to mark special occasions. It was only fitting that "Go For It" would be written on my 59th birthday cake.

On the afternoon following my party, 19 days after the Whipple surgery, my family and I walked a mile and a half around the lake near our Berkshire home. All were amazed to see me go the distance. After working up an appetite we decided to go out for Chinese food. My digestive system and I readied ourselves for a new test. After wonton soup, spare ribs and pork fried rice, the latter two with less hot mustard than usual, dessert began and fortune cookies were distributed. In our usual routine, we each read our fortune aloud. I cracked my cookie, extracted the little piece of white paper and glanced down to read. When my turn came, all at the table were astonished hear me exclaim, "Go For It". Here was another sign the Universe was aligned behind me!!

Chapter 11

My High School Football Reunion: Revisiting the Past

> *"It would be the greatest if you walked into Shea Stadium and we all saw you"*, Josh Z., CaringBridge.org guest message, August 29, 2007.

The first reunion of my Samuel J. Tilden High School football team was held in 2004 in a skybox at Shea Stadium reserved by one of my teammates who later became an official of the NY Mets. On that festive evening, I reunited with many guys I hadn't seen or spoken to in forty years and others with whom I'd made occasional contact. Hair was sparser and bellies bigger but the personalities and team spirit were the same as ever! You really learn a lot from high school reunions. It's surprising how much older everyone looks…except you!!!

Football memories dominated that first reunion and enough of the old spirit and camaraderie developed that we decided to meet each year. Over the next couple of years, the tenor of our meetings gradually morphed from football to our old neighborhoods and memories of the crazy things we did in high school and then to friendship and our present lives. Struggles with health and other serious issues began to surface. Several of my old buddies mentioned bouts with various cancers and other life threatening conditions. I was glad to see how well they looked and that after recovering they had returned to active and productive lives. But being honest, I must say that when I was cancer free, healthy and strong, I was not very interested in the details of what my teammates experienced during their health crises. To that point, I had never been seriously ill and, by golly, I was certain I never would be. Little did I know that at our reunion in 2007, when I was in the throes of my own cancer struggle, I'd be super eager to hear every facet of their stories.

Before our first football reunion, the last time I sat in Shea Stadium was on the afternoon of December 29, 1968 when Joe Namath threw three touchdown passes to lead the NY Jets over the Oakland Raiders 27-23 for the AFL Championship. The Jets' victory paved the way for Broadway Joe's legendary Super Bowl performance to upset the NFL's Baltimore Colts a few weeks later. On the night of that championship game, I worked the graveyard shift – 12 mid-night to 8 AM - loading trucks on the Brooklyn waterfront.

What an incredible experience! It was pitch black and freezing cold and a few of my college buddies and I worked like hell together with the "regulars"…some of the biggest and toughest looking guys we'd ever seen. We were given a couple of large pallets of refrigerators and other massive items and told to load them all in a certain time. The boxes were impossibly heavy. Proper technique was critical to minimize wasted effort and to avoid wrenching your back, crushing your fingers or smashing your toes. In other words, you had to work hard, fast and smart to get the job done, stay injury free and earn the double-time pay provided for night labor. I was an unskilled rookie, so in terms of brute physical exertion, this night was even tougher for me than the two practices a day we did the week before each high school football season. About halfway through the night, I was dead-tired and truly did not know how I'd be able to finish. As the hours passed and I grew wearier, I became less careful, made more incorrect lifts and shoves, and paid for it with aches, pains and bruises to various parts of my body.

You had to admire the "regulars". These guys were professionals. Strong, skillful and stoic, they were dependent on this job for their living. On the other hand, we were college kids looking for some spending money and a little adventure. We were in awe of the "regulars" but extremely grateful we were not headed toward this line of work.

I'm glad I listened to my mother...

Both my parents left school after the eight grade. Theirs was not an easy life. My mother often said, "Get an education. Work with your brain instead of the sweat of your back. Your father is a taxi driver because he didn't go to school. Don't end up like him". My dad spent most of his time in the taxicab and very little with me. He'd get up about 5 each morning and leave the house long before I awoke. Usually, he wouldn't be home again until 6 PM. Dinner was brief and, with his habitual shot of whisky followed by a beer chaser, he'd quickly be asleep, I'd be out playing basketball, or both. I longed for a real relationship with him. Because he was constantly in the cab, I asked several times if we could spend a day together on the job. As an adult, I realized why my dad never said yes. He wasn't too proud of his occupation and didn't want me to end up like him.

My mother was a traditional housewife of the 1950's. Mostly, she cooked, cleaned, ironed, washed and shopped for food. Since this was before electronic bill pay and our family did not keep a checking account, she also dealt with the gas, phone and electric bills by taking trolley car rides to the various utility companies to stand on line and pay the bills in cash. To supplement my father's income, after I turned 10, my mother began working part-time as a cashier in neighborhood stores.

Mom and dad in the 1950's.

Most of my early life was spent in the schoolyards, streets and parks of my East Flatbush, Brooklyn neighborhood playing all manner of sports and physically active games. Because most Brooklyn neighborhoods were solidly lower middle-class, many kids grew up in similar circumstances to mine and sports were a common outlet. In the borough's ethnic communities of the 1950's and 60's, each neighborhood had its local heroes and legends and any sports-minded boy worth his salt aspired to enter the oral pantheon of native athletes.

Because I enjoyed sports and an active social life with many male and female friends, most memories of my youth in East Flatbush are pleasant ones. My neighborhood did, however, acquire a dangerous edge during the last years I lived there. Our apartment was on the top floor of a three story walk-up building and some weekend nights I'd come home very late. To get to the stairs, I had to walk down a long corridor and there was a landing behind the bottom of the staircase near an exit to the backyard that was never locked. In those years, there were incidents in the neighborhood where people were "jumped" and robbed and/or killed by thugs waiting on similar landings behind staircases. Because of this, many times I walked down the corridor toward the staircase all pumped up and ready to fight for my life. I had no idea then that 40 years later I would be fighting for my life against pancreatic cancer, a thuggish disease.

As I made my way through high school and college, my brother Phil, who was 15 years older, was settled into retail middle management and married life. Phil grew up similarly athletic and sports oriented. He had graduated from high school, taken a few college courses and then entered the full time work world.

*My dad, brother Phil and me in our old
neighborhood in the late 1950's.*

As the first of my close relatives to graduate from college, I certainly did not follow a scripted path…

Going to school was fun and interesting but something of an enigma. It was really cool to learn lots of interesting facts and read a ton of books, especially history and biographies of famous people. Many of my teachers were very bright, well schooled and well traveled intellectuals. They also offered great information about how to live in that era and about life in general. If you were smart enough to sort it all out, you could carry away some useful nuggets likely to apply to your own situation.

The enigma of my early education was that, as I progressed through my teenage years, I still enjoyed school and was smart enough to do well and often excel, but I never fully understood why studying a number of specific subjects was going to be important for my life. Because of this, I was either smart enough or, depending on how you look at it, stupid enough, not to take school too seriously. In short, I became a "cherry picker". I barely studied the subjects I was not interested in and, for those I really liked, I found ways to make the work seem like a game so it could be made enjoyable. My parents certainly could not explain the importance of what I should have been studying to me. Because they quit school so young, they were just thrilled I was there!

And, I was there (there I was!), but basically, I continued because it was fun and I did well. The truth was, I had terrible study habits and no discipline whatsoever to wrestle with more difficult subjects that I really wasn't interested in. One subject I particularly hated was science, an odd thing to hear from a person who spent virtually his entire professional life excelling at the science of human physiology. How could my parents, who were barely educated and scraping by to survive, have directly contributed to my late evolving love of science?

High school was all about having fun, enjoying my social life, and playing on the football and baseball teams. Along the way I became vice-president of the school and was voted most popular in my senior class of 1100 students. However, through college, sports and fitness stayed my primary focused interest. My body was my temple, and given what little information was available to the general public in the 1950s and 60s, I took reasonably good care of it. I never smoked, didn't take drugs and limited myself mostly to an occasional beer while in college. Actually at age 14, I had somehow realized too much fat wasn't good for me and to my parents amazement, from then on I only drank skim milk.

STEVEN LEWIS

Me (far right), on official duty as school vice-president.

In the early 1970's, around the time I started my exercise physiology studies at Columbia and Stanford, Dr. Ken Cooper published his groundbreaking book on the benefits of physical fitness called "Aerobics". Before Cooper's book became popular, it was highly unusual to see anyone running outdoors for health or fitness. With my athletic background, and as someone who was interested in exercise for health, fitness and a career, I very much enjoyed running through the quiet streets in my fiancée's suburban neighborhood. To me it was no big deal...I didn't realize I was at the forefront of what would become a world-wide shift in consciousness about the human body's requirement for vigorous movement as a key aspect of health. The reaction of stunned onlookers to my habitual trotting always was the same: "Why is he running, where is he going, why doesn't he just drive? He must be some kind of nut!" When I've recently mentioned this to students and other younger people, they are amazed to hear about the primitive "prehistoric" days without joggers, cyclists, rollerbladers and other aerobics enthusiasts filling streets, parks and playgrounds.

Ironically, as health and fitness became the focus of my career training, life's tragic events took my parents in the opposite direction. In early December 1969, I was at home alone when I heard a knock at the door and saw a policeman standing there. Even before he spoke, I could sense the purpose of his visit. "Your father's taxicab was held up at gunpoint today", he said. Your dad was shot and I'm very sorry to tell you he is gone". Within an hour my brother picked me up and we delivered the heartbreaking news to our mother. We arranged for neighbors to stay with her and my brother and I drove to the morgue to identify our father's body. Of course, losing my dad when I was 21 was a tough break, especially because I never really got to know him.

My father's violent death was a major turning point. Soon after, my thoughts coalesced around the idea of escaping from this tragedy, from my difficult upbringing and from life in Brooklyn, which really was all I knew. Within the next 18 months, I completed my master's degree from Columbia and headed to Palo Alto, California to study for a Ph.D. in exercise physiology at Stanford University. It was the beginning of a new life in a sunnier and warmer place and, in those days before the Silicon Valley exploded, in the rural charm that still enveloped the Stanford campus. Three years into my studies, in the midst of an intense biochemistry course, I received a phone call from my brother. "Mom's circulation is bad", he said. "She has no blood flow to some of her toes and she's in danger of rupturing her aorta". Surgery was scheduled and within a few days, my wife and I were on a 6-hour flight to the hospital in Brooklyn. All effort, however, was futile. The attempt to repair my mom's aorta was fruitless because her surgeons found extensive pancreatic cancer that had already spread to her liver. Within a few months, my mother passed away.

My six years in California, followed by a year doing physiology research in Denmark and twelve years on the medical school faculty at the University of Texas, marked a nearly two decade lapse in contact with many old friends from the east coast. After moving to Boston to work at Boston University in 1990, there were many opportunities to renew ties with friends and acquaintances from my past…

My yearly high school football reunion had been scheduled at Shea Stadium for about one month after my Whipple surgery and two weeks after my birthday. From exchanges of e-mails and from my CaringBridge.org website, many of my teammates knew of my illness and extensive surgery and, I'm sure, were prepared to see "death walking" when I appeared. Instead, I "fooled them". Even though my appearance wasn't exactly "macho", I still received a number of compliments for looking remarkably well and fit for someone who'd been through such recent trauma.

For me, the reunion was an exciting time…my first bit of traveling and extensive socializing since I became ill. For the occasion, I definitely pushed aside my fatigue and was ready to party!

Because of my recent surgery, I'd been exhausted and not very talkative at my surprise birthday party only two weeks before. For this reason, the football reunion really was my first public outing where I shared the details of my illness. I also focused intently on the stories related by my old teammates about surviving cancer and other life threatening conditions. As I was still facing months of treatments, it was simply awesome to listen to the details of their bouts with thyroid cancer, face and mouth cancer, colon cancer, a kidney tumor, Hodgkin's disease, coronary bypass surgery and surviving radiation and chemotherapy. Even though they didn't look ready to play a single set of downs, they were standing in front of me alive, upbeat and doing some of the same goofy stuff they did 40 years ago. The great hope and inspiration received from my teammates reinforced the value of opening up about my cancer diagnosis that began with my Berkshire neighbors and my CaringBridge.org website. Yes, it is possible, in spite of much disease-related turmoil and discomfort to survive, smile, and proceed with a normal life. Grasping all this was one more building block of the positive attitude that held me aloft and radiated to others throughout my cancer journey. The uplift I gave to others lifted me even higher…and so proceeded the cycle of positive energy.

At one of our Tilden High School football team reunions.
I'm the tall guy in the white jersey, rear center.

Chapter 12

CyberKnife Radiation:
Our Hope for a Cure

"The force is with you. The force is all of us who are your team. We are present and accounted for." Bev H. CaringBridge.org, Guest message, October 3, 2007

"I felt like I was on a star trek/space odyssey movie set. Steven was lying on a mattress pillow molded to his body with red lines beaming on him in a graph-like pattern and a robot next to him…that pointed at his tattooed abdomen highlighting the spot to target. The doctors think Steven is likely to be cured so we …feel privileged to be living in a time when this treatment (CyberKnife) is possible." Karen Lewis, CaringBridge.org, journal entry, October 4, 2007.

Soon after the pathology report from Dr. Callery, about 7 days after the Whipple surgery, I was discharged from the hospital and Karen drove me home. Her head was spinning. In spite of confidence in our surgeon and Beth Israel Deaconess Medical Center, her husband's life was at stake. She wanted to confirm that CyberKnife radiation was the best way to treat my remaining cancer. With my physiology background, I normally handled most family medical issues. This time it was different. Extensive surgery and medication had sapped my energy. Karen took charge of Googling cancer of the portal vein and read all she could. She hunted obsessively for other medical centers and experts in Whipple surgery and residual pancreatic cancer. After an exhaustive search, Karen identified the Mayo Clinic and Johns Hopkins School of Medicine for second opinions. Through personal contacts, we spoke directly with Johns Hopkins and Mayo Clinic experts and were told that the surgery I had and the follow-up with CyberKnife radiation was the best possible choice of treatment and that Beth Israel had the expertise we needed.

After all this effort, Karen and I realized that staying on course with treatment at Beth Israel was the right alternative. We then met the radiologists and oncologists to plan the entire course of therapy. The plan called for CyberKnife radiation early in October, 6 weeks of conventional radiation of my abdomen beginning a week later and, after the first of the year,12 weeks of intravenous chemotherapy. After these meetings, Karen and I felt for the first time we had entered the true world of cancer.

Dr. Mahadevan, the radiation oncologist specializing in Cyberknife technology explained the procedure to Karen and I. It was very hi-tech. I would first have a CATscan to mark the precise location of the remaining cancer cells. Two days later, I would undergo the Cyberknife procedure, itself. This involved lying in a dark room for over an hour while the robotic arm of the CyberKnife circled over me and sent high intensity blasts of radiation from every conceivable angle toward the few remaining cancer cells. Cyberknife technology had successfully destroyed inoperable tumors of the brain and nervous system. However, for pancreatic cancer the Cyberknife was still an experimental procedure. So far, in Dr. Mahadevan's hands, the technique was highly successful. All patients with my specific condition - a few cancer cells left after Whipple surgery - who'd been treated by CyberKnife had no tumor recurrence two to four years later. For pancreatic cancer, the first 2 years after treatment are most risky, the risk drops a great deal after that and after 5 years without a recurrence patients are considered cured. CyberKnife radiation promised to be a major breakthrough in treating pancreatic cancer and Dr. Mahadevan's words gave Karen and I great hope that I would, in fact, be cured.

The "hope factor" of the CyberKnife treatment was so great I wrote a CaringBridge.org journal entry requesting that my healing community send all its positive energy at the set appointment time to assist the CyberKnife in doing its job. When I was laying down for the CyberKnife treatment, I visualized all the positive energy coming from my friends and relatives. At the same time, Karen visualized all our relatives and friends standing up, looking in the direction of Boston and beaming all their positive energy to help the CyberKnife.

In spite of all her hope that day, leaving me in the CyberKnife room was one of the few times Karen "lost it" completely during my entire cancer journey. Seeing her husband alone in a dark room with a robotic arm beaming radiation at him absolutely terrified her. When Karen broke down outside the CyberKnife room, the nurse told her it was a normal reaction to seeing a loved one undergo this futuristic procedure.

"My feelings about the procedure were complete confidence that I am cured. I am highly inspired to complete my remaining radiation and chemotherapy treatments", Steven Lewis, CaringBridge.org journal entry one hour following the CyberKnife procedure.

Chapter 13

Taking Care of My Caretaker

"The constant reality is that I have a husband who is fighting cancer", Karen Lewis, CaringBridge.org, journal entry, November 3, 2007.

Anyone who is going through prolonged treatment for a serious illness would love to have an indefatigable caretaker, one who is ever-present with enormous emotional, spiritual and physical nurturing. I was lucky to have such a caretaker in the form of my "beautiful bride" and loving wife, Karen.

Watching Karen maneuver me through this illness while she also balanced her business, our household and her own personal time to cool down was an example of deftness, grace and poise nothing short of seeing Karl Wallenda with tightrope and pole traversing Niagara falls. She literally was amazing…dealing with all aspects of my care and necessary communications with doctors, nurses, compassionate friends and relatives, her elderly parents, and even Verizon (who was more than two weeks late with installing her business phones) etc, etc.

How Karen did all this is an unexplainable mystery of life that leaves no visible trace. You won't see the detailed wonder of her work on the Nature channel or find her achievements in the World Almanac or Guinness book of records. Her presence was a spiritual force that nurtured me, ensured my well being and underwrote that all would move forward in a positive direction. What a remarkable person to have in your corner when slugging it out with pancreatic cancer!

The incredible thing, though, is that my adverse health did not suddenly marshal Karen into high gear, super hero mode. The fact is, that it's *always* been that way, from the moment we met (me 21, she 20) and fell in love in the amazing summer of 1969. That summer the Woodstock music festival took place, Americans walked on the moon for the first time and the New York Mets, until then the doormat of baseball, were on their way to winning the World Series. Karen and I spent that summer together at a camp in Pennsylvania's Pocono mountains. It began like a dream: this beautiful blonde came practically out of nowhere, kissed me goodnight in front of a nature shack full of donkey manure and then a few days later told me she wanted to marry me. Karen's loving force just swept over me and drew me close to her.

Karen and I at Camp Tioga, Lake Como, PA, 1969.

Even in the first days of our relationship, there was little or no chit-chat or small talk. From day one, it was something like, Karen: "Well, I have this really close, loving family... parents, brother, grandparents, aunts, uncles and cousins (and she proceeded to describe everyone in great detail). As soon as camp is over, I really want you to meet all of them"; Me: "Yeah okay, that would be nice". I had never, ever met any girl like this and was totally blown away...definitely aware that something very new and different had entered my life but not really sure of what it was. Then, after only 4 days together, came Karen's stunning pronouncement: "I have something very important to ask you", she said, "and I want a definite "yes" or "no" answer. Are you interested in marrying me?" "Yes", I answered, without hesitation. Karen's overwhelming tide of love had lifted me to a place I never dreamed of. In the face of all this, I was helplessly swept away.

I couldn't help thinking this was the adventure of a lifetime and I was only too eager to grab a ride on the whirlwind called Karen. One thing is for sure - it's never been dull. Adventure, opportunity and excitement have been the name of the game.

And truly a whirlwind Karen was and is - daring enough to take a chance on a raw Brooklyn kid like me who had lots of rough edges and still, to this day, has a few left to work on. So what made this relationship work? A well-off girl from a loving family in the suburbs and a hard scrabble city guy who basically grew up in the streets. For me, one big attraction was the intrigue with our differences. Karen was practical, common-sensed and worldly and I, a dreamer, theorist and neighborhood guy. In spite of these differences, the common thread was strong - same ethnic and religious background, same core values. Another big plus was that Karen and I always shared a similar, well-developed sense of humor. She was and remains ever ready to laugh loudly at my silly jokes and pranks.

To put Karen's remarkable effort during my year with cancer into proper perspective, you should know she has never been a "stay-at-home wife" and, while I struggled with my illness and the effects of the treatments, she was not hovering around me immediately catering to my every need. In fact, while taking care of me, Karen continued to run her own successful office furniture business. Also during my illness, Karen and her partners launched a separate new non-profit entity that provides charitable groups with office furniture from corporate America ("Corporate castoffs for a cause", Boston Globe, Sept 7, 2008). And how, you may ask, did this superwoman accomplish all this business while at the same time providing caretaking that made Florence Nightingale look like Leona Helmsley? Well, a key factor responsible for all of Karen's success is her highly energetic and positive nature. She also is blessed with a high level of emotional intelligence… she is adept at sensing her own feelings and those of her family members and instinctively behaves appropriately. In spite of her superhuman strengths and achievements, Karen's emotional intelligence can, however, be her "Achilles heel". Her very sensitive, nurturing soul is easily seduced by the troubles of others. Karen's tender soul was, of course, particularly vulnerable to her husband of 37 years' life threatening illness. Of course, no one is perfect and there were occasions when Karen would lose patience with my cancer-driven neediness. Some times I'd take advantage by complaining, "Don't be mean to a cancer patient" in a sniveling whiney voice". The first few times I tried this Karen would respond by going the extra mile to make me feel more comfortable. However, as the year rolled on my whining complaint simply became a recurring source of needed humor.

*Karen and I, posing for her company's Boston Globe
article, one year after my Whipple surgery.*

In fact, as Karen and I first mapped our strategy to
navigate my cancer journey, we implicitly understood that
continuing our humorous ways would help keep us in the
best of spirits. Laughter had always been a vital part of our
teamwork. Because we were determined to keep our lives
as normal as possible, we proceeded to laugh at ourselves
and at all the crazy stuff we had to deal with. My humorous
CaringBridge.org journal entries and similar guest message
responses reflected this approach.

There is documented evidence that humor and laughter
can benefit cancer patients and their caretakers (e.g. J. Holland,
"The Human Side of Cancer", Harper, New York, 1999) and
the truth is that Karen and I desperately needed to laugh. My
cancer journey certainly was no cakewalk for either of us. After
Karen was devastated by my cancer diagnosis, she and her
"out-of-body" counterpart experienced a series of particularly
distressing moments. These particularly harrowing moments
included waiting through my 7-hour Whipple surgery, seeing

my surgeon not smiling when he gave us the pathology report, reading bleak facts about pancreatic cancer on Google, leaving me in the CyberKnife procedure room with the star wars-like robot, when I fell and went to the emergency room on Thanksgiving (see Chapter 15), and, after finishing chemo, when my blood test for tumor cell activity was abnormal (see Chapter 17). In spite of Karen's typically indomitable spirit, were it not for our laughter, our determination to stay positive and her ability to go "out of body", all this distress would have had her bouncing off the walls.

In addition to the huge angst my illness created for Karen, a few days after my CyberKnife radiation, she stopped home after a visit to her doctor to tell me she had a lump in her breast that required an ultrasound test, mammogram and biopsy. With all I'd been going through and her own health uncertainty, Karen's fear abounded. When she arrived at the hospital on time for her sonogram and mammogram appointment, she found 20 women waiting ahead of her. My emotionally intelligent wife "lost it" and complained loudly to the supervisor that her husband had pancreatic cancer and she needed to be with him. This outburst got Karen to the front of the line. The reason that Karen "lost it" was that the lump in her breast put a big dent in her own positive attitude. She was terrified that her illness would prevent her from completing her mission of getting me well. Her fear had become too great to contain by her "out of body" emotional dissociation

With Karen possibly having her own health crisis and me feeling all the positive energy I'd been primed with, I instinctively, in spite of facing my own radiation and chemo treatments, volunteered my services as *her* caretaker. What a pair we were: a pancreatic cancer patient and a potential breast cancer patient mutually caring for each other.

Give me a break. Was it really possible for us to do this? Thankfully, we did not have to find out. It took Karen's normal breast biopsy report about 10 days later to subdue our intense fear that our lives were just falling apart.

A key point is that as tough as it is for a cancer patient to cope with his or her own illness, it is also an extremely difficult time for the patient's primary caretaker. Fortunately, I envisioned this very early in my cancer journey. I realized the more positive my attitude and the more of my focused attention I could give to Karen, the more she could find the energy to uncomplainingly care for me and to help keep me in a positive state of mind. Physical and emotional energy are essential requirements for enthusiastic long-term caretaking. As my cancer journey progressed, I tried hard to do the "little things" that kept Karen and I emotionally close and actually added to our relationship during this trying period. For example, borrowing from my surgeon, as much as I could think of it, I took to calling Karen "my beautiful bride". It was not only sweet for Karen to hear this from me but it would remind her of Dr. Callery, the man Karen believed walked on water.

Chapter 14

Cancer and Game 4: Radiation Treatment and the Inspiration of Athletes

> *"Steven, you are really living your sports metaphor— your focus and determination, complete with a love story with the beautiful cheerleader (Karen), a field of dreams in the Berkshires and a first string team of the best family, friends and doctors surrounding you…",* Helen B., CaringBridge.org guest message, November 16, 2007.

As a cancer patient who also is an exercise and sports enthusiast, I realized that my healing community and I shared the same "emotional locker room". Like a sports team, we were all in it together and, I as captain, was assigned to be the positive "go to guy". Analogous to an athlete who is injured, cancer was my "injury". And like athletes whose injuries often are repaired by surgery, my "cancer injury" was "repaired" by my Whipple surgery and the hope-giving CyberKnife radiation. After surgery, athletes proceed through rigorous rehab regimens to return them to game condition fitness and coordination. In my case, radiation treatment followed by chemotherapy was my "rehab" to restore me to health and fitness for resuming a normal life.

My radiation treatments were scheduled for 28 sessions, 5 days per week for 5 and ½ weeks and my radiation doctor told me, "Your full-time job is to get better". For me, getting better meant returning to the robust workouts I routinely performed before my Whipple surgery. I was determined to continue with my regular exercise program but my operation had really taken its toll. As an exercise physiologist, I realized I had to start gradually. So I began again at about 10 to 15 percent of my normal workout and progressively increased from there. As the weeks of radiation passed, I was able to do about 70 percent of my normal exercise routine without overtaxing. These workouts – including cardio and light weightlifting – and the discipline of doing it regularly did wonders for my body and spirit and became as vital a part of my healing regimen as the 25 pills per day I was then taking. Along with the CaringBridge.org guest messages that filled my emotional locker room and the recollection of my paranormal force fields experience, my regular workouts were key elements of a "spiritual insurance policy" that never let me even begin to feel sorry for myself.

Professional athletes pay close attention to how their workouts, diet and rest patterns affect their physical performance. Similarly, as a cancer patient, I found it valuable to focus on my new physiology and how it was affected by my surgery, treatments, medications, diet, exercise and sleep. As my body made the necessary adjustments, I along with it, was tasked to stay in touch, to be correctly informed and to be flexible enough to adapt to whatever needed to be done. This was my mission!

In addition to my exercise workouts, during my period of radiation treatment a new weapon was added to my healing arsenal. At that time, my digestive system was nagging me for help in dealing with foods higher in fat content. This assistance provided by my gastrointestinal specialist were pills to better digest fats and instruction to observe exactly which foods were difficult to digest. Once I began taking these pills and more closely watching the foods I ate, my digestive system and I resumed our once blissful relationship. We now had the potential wherewithal to complete my cancer journey to our mutual gastrointestinal satisfaction.

There was, however, one potential hitch: the chemo pills I took during my radiation treatments. These pills are used to weaken cancer cells and make it easier for radiation to kill them. There are number of possible side effects of the chemo pills, some of which are digestive such as loss of appetite, nausea and vomiting. Several ex-cancer patients told me I would be nauseous and vomit from the radiation and/or chemo. Luckily, I did not have this experience. Aside from some occasional and minor gastric reflux, however, I never became nauseous or vomited during my entire cancer journey. Also, everyone who knows me can attest to the fact that my usually ravenous appetite was undiminished by my cancer treatments. I attribute much of this to being especially conscious not to conjure up negative thoughts. One time I felt I was starting to get nauseous and the more I thought about it the more real it seemed. I then stopped thinking about the nausea and it went away.

Other potential side effects of the radiation/chemo pills were tiredness, weakness, back/joint/muscle pain, headache, dizziness, trouble sleeping, skin darkness or dry and itchy skin. I never read the details of the side effects of any of the treatments. What was the point? The doctors said these side effects vary a lot from person to person. Reading about all the side effects likely would have caused me to dwell on them and that negativity alone could have me feel ill.

Of course, I wish I never had cancer. However, as a sports enthusiast, it was an amazing year to have time to watch your local teams excel: the Boston Red Sox and Celtics won world championships and the New England Patriots went undefeated until the Super Bowl. Seeing all these local victories definitely contributed to keeping me as upbeat as a cancer patient could be. And as a cancer patient, I began to notice and was greatly inspired by the many athletes who overcame cancer and other life-threatening illnesses to excel in their sport.

On October 28th, while in radiation treatment exactly two months after my Whipple surgery, I watched intently as Jon Lester, the young Red Sox pitcher and survivor of non-Hodgkin's lymphoma, started and won the final game – Game 4 - of the World Series. At the same time the year before, Lester was not playing baseball but undergoing chemotherapy. With my own chemotherapy scheduled to begin two months later, watching Jon Lester pitch and win this game was a huge spiritual uplift. Any cancer patient could not help but be moved by the words of Red Sox veteran pitcher Curt Schilling (whose own wife is a melanoma survivor) spoken the day before the final Series game: "Game 4 of the World Series is going to be a whole lot different than had he (Lester) not gone through what he went through. There's no mountain he can't climb, no hurdle he can't jump. It's a challenge for a young pitcher, but at the end of the day, there's nothing he's going to see in Game 4 that…isn't dwarfed by what he's already beaten and overcome." Incredible performance by Lester, remarkable words of Schilling and add to it the illustrious performance of Red Sox third baseman Mike Lowell, a survivor of testicular cancer, who was voted most valuable player of the 2007 World Series. It is difficult to describe how much all this meant to me as I moved forward in my cancer journey!

There are increasing numbers of professional athletes who continued their athletic careers after surviving cancer and other serious illnesses. Some examples are Mark Herzlich, the professional football player who survived bone cancer, Edna

Campbell the WNBA player who returned to pro basketball after breast cancer, Alonzo Mourning, the professional basketball star who underwent a mid-career kidney transplant, hockey star Mario Lemieux, and Andres Galarraga, the baseball star who won the Comeback Player of the Year Award after treatment for non-Hodgkin's lymphoma. Well known is the story of Lance Armstrong, who survived testicular cancer that had spread to his abdomen, lungs and brain.

As captain of my healing team, I remained conscious of keeping positive to lift the spirits of Karen and the rest of my healing teammates. I always did my CaringBridge.org journal entries when I was in good spirits but instead of writing I was feeling "good" I wrote I was doing "great". This "brought my attitude up a notch (i.e., "good" to "great") and I instinctively knew that if I brought it up a notch, I'd get positive feedback brought up a notch from my teammates. It's like being addicted to positive energy. I began to instinctively enjoy the positive energy sent to me by my healing teammates and the more I could inspire people, the more positives I would get in return. It was like winning, the World Series, Super Bowl and NBA championship rolled into one.

Chapter 15

My Bathroom Fall and the "Caretaker Olympics"

> *"Karen and I have used laughter as our therapy to get through this crazy week. There is no better medicine when life seems overwhelming"*, Steven Lewis, CaringBridge.org, journal entry, November 28, 2007.

Three months after my surgery, on the day before Thanksgiving, I reached a key milestone in my cancer ordeal: my 6 weeks of daily radiation treatments were now complete. The chemo pills required as part of these treatments caused unpleasant side effects and I was thrilled to stop taking them. I now looked forward to more than a month away from the hospital, exercising again and trying to live a "normal" life before starting intravenous chemo treatments early in January. Karen also was relieved because she was anxious to have her husband back as a "playmate" again and she yearned for a respite from caretaking.

Our family was preparing for a special holiday. Ryan had spent the last few Thanksgivings with the U.S. Army in Iraq, Germany and Afghanistan, so it was the first Thanksgiving in several years we'd all be together. Karen's parents were flying in from Florida and the three generations truly had a lot to be thankful for. The Universe, however, had other plans for us.

At 4:30 AM Thanksgiving morning, Karen awoke suddenly to a huge thud. She saw I was not in bed and heard me groan from the direction of the bathroom floor. Karen found me stretched out on the floor holding my head in my hands and moaning with a puddle of blood beneath my right foot. My foot hurt terribly but I couldn't move because my head was still spinning. Karen brought me a pillow, eased it under my head and placed a blanket around my body. The bathroom was too small for her to get into position to examine my foot. I needed to get into bed so she could fully inspect the injury. However, I did not want to move until I felt ready to stand.

For about 10 minutes Karen stayed next to me on the bathroom floor and just held my hand. What a pathetic site we were! After all we had been through since late August, both of us desperately ached for this upcoming month break from clinics, doctors and treatments. We wanted no further life challenges to hurdle right now...we needed a rest!

When I regained my composure, I got up, hobbled into bed and flopped down taking care not to let my foot touch anything along the way. Now Karen was able to see the damage to my foot. I knew by the look on her face I was not in store for a routine fix of band aids and Bactine!

Karen wanted to call 911 but after daily radiation treatments for 6 weeks, I was not interested in visiting a hospital. I hoped to just clean up my foot, bandage it and let it heal at home. She looked at me and said, "Steven, we MUST go to the emergency room, this wound is too deep." I kept challenging her until I sat up at the edge of the bed and crossed my leg at the knee so I could view the bottom of my foot.

I stared in amazement as I saw down past several layers of skin nearly to the muscles of my foot by the base of the big toe. Almost every layer of skin was pushed aside over a 3"x3" squared area and it continued down the middle of the foot. So much for slate floors! When I fainted, I had unconsciously tried to get traction on the slate with my big toe and the skin below it. As a side effect of the chemo pills I had just finished, the skin of my foot was brittle and easily torn by the roughness of the floor.

Karen couldn't properly clean the wound. It was too deep and definitely needed medical attention. She wrapped my foot in a towel, sealed the towel with tape, helped me get dressed, put my arm around her neck, got me up, hopped me to the car and off we went…another trip to our local hospital in the Berkshires.

So there I was in the same room, in the same hospital as the night I turned yellow three months before! As I lay there on the gurney, the doctor unwrapped the towel from my foot and examined it. "Gosh, how did you ever do this", he exclaimed before I related my tale of woe. As he gently touched the tender spots, I nearly hit the emergency room ceiling. Because of the deepness and extreme sensitivity of the wound, I needed intravenous knockout sedation while it was treated. While I lay unconscious for several minutes, the doctor and two nurses worked feverishly to clean, disinfect and bandage the areas of detached skin. Before I left the hospital I was given painkillers and antibiotics and told my foot would take a few weeks to heal. There I was, on my sojourn between radiation and chemotherapy, a patient once again.

As you can imagine, our Thanksgiving dinner did not go exactly as anticipated. In spite of the other plans the Universe had for us, we were truly thankful my head missed the granite countertop of my bathroom sink when I fell. My cancer and treatments had already put Karen through too much stress. After my fall she wondered if she'd be a finalist in the "caretaker Olympics" or if any insane asylums specialized in cancer caretakers that have lost their minds.

To top it off, a few weeks later, while my foot was still healing, Karen awoke one morning feeling the room swirling rapidly around her. She had developed a severe case of vertigo and could not walk without assistance. After a few frantic phone calls to help my hysterical caretaker, a relative who is an ear, nose and throat specialist prescribed the Epply maneuver. This is a vertigo treatment that calls for hanging your head off a bed in several different positions. So here we were: a pancreatic cancer patient between radiation and chemo treatments with a foot bandaged in "mummy-mode" trying to help his caretaker who was "spinning out of control".

In a couple of days, The Epply manuever had reduced Karen's sensation of severe swirling to that of merely a rocking boat…I was no longer married to a "dizzy" blonde. Karen's walking was now much improved although I still stayed behind her with hands on her hips in conga line fashion. With one partner with an unsteady gait and another with a skinless foot, it was, however, hard to coordinate the conga "one, two, three, kick".

Chapter 16

Intravenous Chemotherapy: My Toughest Physical Challenge

> *"Two days ago, I had my first of twelve I.V. chemo treatments…My doctors told me I might experience fatigue, fever and nausea for the first couple of days after treatment. So I slept for a while when I got home. If I had my choice of side effects, I'll take a nap anytime…As we gallop along together on the road to excellent health, Karen now affectionately calls me her "chemo-sabi"*, Steven Lewis, CaringBridge. org, journal entry, January 5, 2008.

As snow coated Boston and the Berkshires in late December and the first few days of January, I readied myself to begin 12 intravenous chemo treatments. My schedule called for one treatment per week for three weeks, the following week off and this sequence repeated four times over a 3-month period. I wasn't too concerned about beginning I.V. chemo. After all, I had tolerated radiation fairly well. After hearing stories of radiation misery from others, my radiation treatments that ended about one month earlier were much less taxing than expected. The radiation and the chemo pills that went with it didn't bother me too much. I was able to exercise regularly, wasn't nauseous and didn't vomit. I attributed this to being otherwise in good health prior to my cancer diagnosis and to always keeping in good physical shape. I figured I'd tolerate weekly chemo treatments about the same. So as I drove to the hospital on January 4th for my first I.V chemo treatment, I was generally upbeat and looking forward to putting this last phase of my cancer therapy behind me.

My chemo treatments took place in a big open room with many reclining chairs and beds in the hospital's cancer unit. All of the staff - doctors, nurses and aids - were extremely friendly, kind and helpful. About 25 patients received chemo treatments at any one time. This differed drastically from my earlier radiation treatments in which I was the only person in a pleasant wood paneled room. Radiation treatments took only 15 minutes and there were no IVs required. Except for a brief wait before each radiation treatment, I did not see other cancer patients. In contrast, in the large open room where I received chemo treatment there were many sickly patients some of whom were alone and others tended to by family members. Several had lost their hair and were wearing hats, wigs or bandanas. As I received the intravenous chemo fluids and watched and listened to other patients nearby I felt more like a real cancer patient than I did at any time during my journey. The intensity of this feeling would increase dramatically as the weeks of chemo treatment wore on and my side effects mounted.

For me, chemotherapy was a much different ballgame than radiation. Because of the treatment atmosphere and side effects, chemotherapy was much more psychologically and physically taxing. My caretaker felt similarly. Karen accompanied me to a few of my radiation treatments but never came with me to a single chemo treatment. "As long as you're okay to drive back and forth", she said "there's no reason for me to come unless you really want me to". After I completed chemo, Karen admitted she was extremely reluctant to watch toxic fluids drain into my body and to see very sickly people receive similar treatment.

In spite of never getting nauseous, never vomiting and not losing a hair from my head (although I did lose some from limbs and torso) getting through chemo was the hardest physical challenge of my life. I started out determined to exercise regularly, as I'd done through most of my radiation treatment. After recovering from my fall and skinned foot, I'd returned to reasonable physical shape during the 6-week break between radiation and chemo. So the morning after my very first I.V. chemo treatment, I decided to put myself through a strenuous workout. I felt fine for the rest of that day and the next morning but the next afternoon and evening was spent in bed with fever and chills and a severe itchy rash developed over my entire body. What a shock to my system! As the first few chemo treatments progressed, I gingerly exercised a few more times but extreme fatigue took an increasing toll on my ability to workout.

As the 12 weeks of treatment passed, my fatigue progressively increased. I became anemic, my immune system was compromised and I napped longer and more frequently during the day. My itchy rash continued unabated. After 7 to 8 weeks of treatment, I'd spend a couple of days in bed with fever and chills following exercise workouts. This became much too unpleasant so, in early March about a month before completing chemo, I stopped working out. Instead, as March progressed, I napped longer and longer each day. On many days, I started napping right after breakfast and a number of times it seemed I'd simply just wake up to greet my wife and son, eat and then go right back to sleep. I called this period my Rip Van Winkle mode. The sleeping actually helped my itchy rash…you don't scratch when you sleep. Also, as long as I wasn't nauseous and didn't vomit, napping was not an objectionable side effect. The only thing is, with me asleep, my beautiful bride became very lonely and took to cooking as her chosen therapy. One of Karen's favorite recipes was her grandma's chicken matzo ball soup. This soup originated in Poland over 100 years ago and, according to oral history, long before chemo was developed eating this soup was an "integral part" of cancer fighting.

Also, around this time, the chemo was causing dramatic impairment of my mental alertness. In this state I called "chemo-brain", clear thinking was difficult, if not impossible. It was as if a big cloud washed over me and brought a wave of tiredness that left me awake but really not present...kind of like being at Woodstock in 1969. Chemo-brain also was a very frustrating side effect for Karen because she felt I really wasn't there for her. When you combine chemo-brain with sleeping a lot, it seemed to Karen that I hardly was around. I suggested Karen take some drugs and join me on my chemo trip but she still had to focus on being my designated driver.

Karen and Mindy share the same birthday in March and they insisted I be present and look rested for several planned birthday celebrations. Buying cards and flowers and attending dinners with family and friends sapped virtually all my energy. I napped mornings and afternoons, but always managed to awaken in time to fully partake in all significant events. After partying, I'd resume my horizontal position. Partying, sleeping and partying again really was pretty cool...I've been told it's the rock star lifestyle.

I'd never performed volunteer service at a hospital and throughout my chemotherapy I was totally in awe of Beth Israel's cancer unit volunteers. Each was a cancer survivor whose job it was to get whatever you needed - a drink, snack, lunch or something to read - to make you feel more comfortable. As I got to know some of their incredible stories - including one man who survived two different types of cancer and a liver cancer patient, who after his liver transplant, returned to hard physical labor as a roofer - I was inspired to seriously consider volunteering my own time once I was cured. However, as began my last weeks of chemo treatment, I was totally fed up and volunteer work with cancer patients became the last possible thing I aspired to. I couldn't wait to get the chemo behind me, leave that place and never come back!

Shortly before noon on April 10, 2008, the last of my chemo fluid dripped in, my I.V. was removed and I headed - no, "dashed" is the correct word - out of Beth Israel's cancer unit. Chemo was now in my rearview mirror. After a quick but emotional call to Karen, I bounded off for a low-key but personally meaningful celebration; lunch of whitefish salad on a bagel, a short walk in the park with dog Leeza in glorious weather and a much longer chemo-induced nap.

After I awoke, I thought to myself, "The end of chemo means I'll soon be getting back my old energy. I'll give it three or four weeks and then I'll gradually resume a regular fitness program. Those stories I heard about people taking many months to regain their strength and stamina don't apply to me. I was very active before so it won't be long before I'll be my old in-shape self." Boy was I surprised. The chemo had really challenged my immune system. For a few weeks after stopping chemo treatments, my daytime sleeping, i.e. Rip Van Winkle mode, and chemo brain were almost as much as during chemo, itself. I really had thought that soon after my treatments were over, I would rapidly bounce back with all my old energy. Instead, even though my chemo treatments were in my rearview mirror, my low energy level and chemo brain often rode shotgun along with me for a few more months.

My beautiful caretaker and me sharing a special moment near our Berkshire home during the summer following my chemotherapy.

Chapter 17

A Rollercoaster Ride from Positive to Negative and Back Again

> *"The silver lining of the gloomy cloud you endured enabled you to think about and gain renewed appreciation for all the blessings you've had in your life."*...Everett H., CaringBridge.org guest message, May 20, 2008.

Over my 9-month journey through the cancer diagnosis, surgery, CyberKnife, radiation and chemo I gained great confidence I would be a cancer survivor. Because of this, I was shocked that in spite of clean CAT scan results early in May 2008, I also was told my blood tested abnormally high for CA 19-9, a biomarker of pancreatic tumor activity. The fact that my CA 19-9 levels had normalized after 99% of my tumor was surgically removed and then stayed normal had been a very positive factor. However, the newly elevated CA 19-9 put Karen and I into a major tailspin!!! What this meant was, that in spite of all I'd endured, I was potentially facing - not immediately or very soon, but certainly much too prematurely - a face-to-face meeting with the "spirit in the sky". My very positive attitude received a major dent when I got this news and though Karen tried her best to break my funk, my bad mood ended-up bringing her down, too.

Just as my positive thinking was contagious to this point in my cancer journey, I now saw clearly by Karen's growing depression, the detrimental effects of my recent negative attitude. I was not eager to have all the positive energy created during my journey suddenly collapse in a heap on the basis of one laboratory test. Because of this, Karen and I did not widely share my abnormal blood test results. I also was reluctant to announce my blood findings on my CaringBridge.org website. The fact was, while I waited for results of a repeat blood test to verify the abnormality, I was fighting my negative attitude with hopes that laboratory findings are sometimes incorrect. This could be because of a mistake in the testing lab's analysis. I did, however, question the likelihood of such a mistake at a reputable lab connected with a hospital of Harvard Medical School. Another possibility was that the CA19-9 results were a fluke related to my very recently stopping chemotherapy. We had heard instances of similar mistakenly abnormal tests in patients soon after chemo. Actually, my instincts coming from many years experience as a physiologist suggested that the appearance of the abnormal blood result was suspicious in its timing because my CA19-9 had stayed normal during my entire treatment regimen. On the other hand, I had had no previous professional experience with cancer treatments or CA19-9 levels.

To help us cope while waiting for the repeat test results, Karen and I spent several days searching our souls. Why might my cancer be returning and what would this mean in the big picture of our lives? We cried, and thought and talked a great deal about the power of family, the special gifts we've been blessed with as individuals and all the hard work we've done through the years to make things right for our selves and our children. What emerged was something I termed the "value-added" effect of my life. This involved consciously recognizing and putting into words my life's intrinsic value... what was most unique and special about the life I've lived. In other words, defining my life's value-added effect involved simply and concisely spelling out any small but meaningful benefit my existence brought to the world. In essence, my life's intrinsic value involved two factors. Firstly, my presence added a great deal that was unique and positive to our family relationships and, if I were absent, my wife and children would very deeply miss my contributions. Secondly, I realized that I was blessed with a special gift of being able to figure out complicated things and to express them in a simplified form easily understandable to others.

When I was forced to consider, more directly and imminently than ever before, my own mortality, verbalizing my life's value gave meaning to my existence and provided a tremendous spiritual uplift. Expressing this to Karen instantly created a wave of good feeling coursing through me. My mental images were quite vivid, although somewhat corny. What I visualized was a "smiley face" - like the "have a good day" face ubiquitous in the 1970's and the Emoticons of today - in my chest and abdomen that returned me to a very positive state of mind.

And then, in a couple days, came the most fabulous phone message I've ever received…"Hello, Steven. This is Dr. Schwarzberg. You'll be happy to know your CA 19-9 is back down to 18, which is within the normal range. The last one probably was just a fluke. Hope you have a wonderful cruise." Wheeeewh!!! That evening, my beautiful bride and I celebrated joyously over dinner with margaritas at our favorite Mexican restaurant. After returning home we watched the Red Sox's Jon Lester – the cancer survivor who pitched the final game of the previous World Series – throw a no-hitter against the Kansas City Royals. We looked forward eagerly to our Adriatic cruise starting in the next ten days and, more importantly, that we'd be vacationing with me in apparently good health. Our level of inspiration was never higher!

This episode with my changing blood test result provides important insight into the significance of maintaining a positive attitude for maximizing quality of life during illness. The insight came when our attitudes turned from positive to negative on the basis of what turned out to be a falsely abnormal test result. In this case, soon after I became negative, so did Karen, and the reciprocal flow of positive attitude that had swirled between us all year quickly became a reciprocal flow of negative energy. The few days we spent waiting for the repeat test result were among the toughest I've ever faced. Though it was a traumatic few days, the painful process we went through to regain our positive outlook was remarkably fulfilling and put many life-issues into context as I traveled the road back to excellent health.

Chapter 18

Bon Voyage: Cancer in Our Wake

> *"You must plan a cruise immediately. This is absolutely required for a complete recovery"*, Sheila G., CaringBridge.org guest message, October 3, 2007.

Karen and I had always dreamed of visiting Greece and cruising through its magnificent islands. As my cancer treatment drew to a close, this seemed a great way to celebrate its conclusion. We scheduled our voyage to begin 6 weeks after my final chemotherapy session. This would provide me some pre-cruise recovery of energy prior to embarking.

Along with our cruise through the Greek islands, Karen and I felt the need to symbolically mark the end of my last remnants of cancer and my return to a healthy life. As it turned out, the symbolic event we planned revolved around a fleece, but *not* a golden fleece like the one Jason sought in Greek mythology.

As my year as a cancer patient wore on, Karen grew weary of returning from work and viewing me huddled in a *green*, zippered fleece – "Big Bird-like" in its fluffiness - that I wore almost daily to protect me from winter drafts and chills that were side effects of my chemo. I hadn't worn the fleece before getting sick but had stumbled on it while puttering around the house during my illness-induced "free time". "Getting rid of that rag", Karen said, "will symbolize your complete recovery from cancer". In response to her repeated urging to permanently dispose of the fleece, I considered a formal garment-burning event in an open field near our home in the Berkshires. However, as plans for our Adriatic cruise firmed up and the time for embarkation grew nearer, our voyage seemed a unique opportunity to drown the said item of clothing.

"Check out that sign", I said to Karen, as we stepped out on the veranda of our cruise stateroom and looked below to the promenade deck: "Do Not Throw Any Objects Overboard". In spite of that explicit directive, we were determined to proceed with our plot to rid ourselves of the olive-colored garment by having it "walk the plank".

Our cruise began with a late afternoon departure from Venice, followed by dinner with our assigned tablemates. After brief introductions, Karen announced that the purpose of our cruise was to celebrate the successful end of my year-long pancreatic cancer ordeal. Remarkably, sitting right beside Karen and I were a father with daughter who was battling Hodgkin's disease (and another daughter lost to brain cancer) and a woman whose husband had very recently succumbed to esophageal cancer.

After a pleasant post-dinner show, Karen and I returned to our stateroom still exhausted from our jet lag and quickly fell sound asleep. At about 3 AM, our off-kilter internal time clocks awoke us and we hungrily ordered room service. We dined on our stateroom veranda under a starry Adriatic sky and outdoor lights that surrounded the promenade deck below and its "do not jettison" sign. As our meal progressed, so did a devilish look in Karen's eye. "Now is the time", she declared, "for you to toss that thing overboard". "I can't", I protested, chickening out of my earlier fleece disposal pledge, "what about the sign." After several exchanges of "Yes, you can... No, I can't", she barked, "OK, just give it to me...I'll do it." And, with that, Karen grabbed the fleece, deftly wrapped in a plastic grocery bag to prevent wind-drift back to the ship and flung it over the promenade and into the dark Adriatic. As it floated away and sank in the ship's wake, my cancer torment found a resting place in Davy Jones' locker.

Enjoying a beer in Athens after climbing the Parthenon a couple months post-chemotherapy.

Chapter 19

A New Beginning

Diagnosed with pancreatic cancer in August of 2007, I had progressed through nine months of intensive cancer treatment – including the dramatic Whipple surgery, experimental CyberKnife radiation, conventional radiation and chemotherapy. My CA-19 tumor marker number was normal and CT scans of my pancreas and other abdominal organs shown no signs of tumors. It was time to progressively regain my physical strength and stamina and begin planning to return to a normal life that included a regular job. With two homes to support, my nine months out of work was wreaking havoc with our finances. Just as important was my own strong desire to return to a productive career.

The decline in physical capacity brought about by prolonged intensive cancer treatment also had major psychological effects. As days, weeks and months following our celebratory cruise passed, I wondered how quickly I would regain my former physical abilities and if, in fact, I would ever fully recover them. Other thoughts also crept in. I was now 60 years old. After a devastating illness of this magnitude, what path should I take in my work life? Could I cope with a full-time job, or would a part-time or temporary job be more appropriate for beginning to work again? Should I restart my long career as a university teacher and researcher or try a new career path, perhaps one that involved some of the new life skills I learned as a cancer patient? While I wrestled with these and many other related issues I began work on this book.

Nearly a year of combined soul-searching and job hunting led to a unique career opportunity to teach physiology to medical students in the West Indies. In April 2009, only one week before leaving for the Caribbean, my oncologists were alarmed when a CAT scan of my liver showed a large, ominous looking object. "You may have to postpone your job plans", they said. As Karen and I were bolted back into fear mode, the doctors quickly scheduled me for an extra full day in the hospital that included two MRI's, a liver ultrasound test and several blood tests. Luckily, the testing did not corroborate a potential abnormality and I arrived on schedule to begin my new job as professor of physiology at the American University of the Caribbean School of Medicine on the Dutch side of St. Maarten. This capped a remarkable transition from death's door to a Caribbean paradise in which I never dreamed I would live.

Part of the view from our St. Maarten apartment.

In my free time, I continued work on this book from the deck of our high-rise apartment not far from the medical school. During breaks from writing, I enjoyed a sweeping vista of mountains, the Simpson Bay lagoon, the town of Marigot in French St. Martin, a stretch of the Caribbean Sea with the nearby island of Anguilla in the background, and the St. Maarten airport and beaches on the Dutch side of the island. It was a very tough job assignment but somebody had to do it!

Chapter 20

Reversal of Fortune

My cancer follow-up was scheduled to include five years of regular CAT scans, MRIs, blood tests and physical exams. For pancreatic cancer, if there is no evidence of cancer recurrence after five years, patients are considered "cured". In April 2010, nearly three years after my Whipple surgery, I returned to Beth Israel Hospital in Boston for my yearly physical exam and routine cancer check-up, riding high on my belief that approaching 3 years cancer-free, I most likely was cured. As it turned out, my yearly physical was scheduled a day after my CAT scan and before I met with my oncologists to review the findings. Karen had accompanied me to my physical that day and we were in the waiting room when my internist, Dr. Jim Heffernan and I exchanged glances as he walked a patient to another room. The look on his face was troubling but I said nothing to Karen.

When Karen and I entered Dr. Heffernan's office, he looked quite uncomfortable. In the many years I'd been his patient, I had never seen him look that way. Even before he spoke, I sensed he'd shortly be giving us terrible news, something usually provided by oncologists much more familiar with the task. Dr. Heffernan conveyed the radiologist's CAT scan report: There was very clear evidence of a tumor in my liver that looked malignant and a biopsy was needed to confirm this. Karen and I quickly exchanged painful looks and words…we were well aware of the likely consequences. Pretty much all Dr. Heffernan could say was, "Well, since your

Whipple surgery, you've had three *good* years. The oncologists know much more about this than I do, so it is best to discuss all the details with them."

My regular oncologist was away with health problems. A substitute from his department exchanged a few quick words with Karen and I when we met with him the next day. He told us that my pancreatic cancer marker blood CA 19-9 levels were much higher than normal, consistent with the CAT scan evidence of a tumor in my liver and that this seemed a likely metastasis of the pancreatic cancer. Absolute confirmation of this would come from results of a liver biopsy he scheduled for 2 days later.

After the liver biopsy, we again met with the substitute oncologist. He confirmed the diagnosis of metastasis to my liver. When Karen and I asked about possible treatments, the oncologist responded by saying, "At this point the best we can offer is palliative care". He then cursorily examined me by flicking his fingers at the glands in my neck and stating without any proof, "It's already in your lymph". Karen and I both knew that palliative care is meant to limit pain and discomfort caused by a terminal illness. We were in total disbelief and refused to accept that nothing else could be done. "What about liver surgery to remove the tumor", we asked. The oncologist gravely stated that spread of pancreatic cancer to the liver is virtually incurable because once it enters the liver it quickly spreads elsewhere. I refused to accept this…this was my life he was dealing with. "How can you know this for sure"?, I asked. "What other test can tell if the tumor is contained or has spread?". He responded by saying that a PET (positron emission tomography) scan could give evidence of tumor containment or spread but the test might not provide definitive results. Karen and I did not know this at the time, but because no patient at

Beth Israel Deaconess Medical Center had ever survived liver metastasis of pancreatic cancer, the oncologist was convinced my fate was sealed. He then told us that PET scans were very expensive and that because the cancer had almost certainly spread out of my liver, the cost of the PET scan might not be justified. There also were significant risks to liver surgery he said, in manner that clearly indicated he was trying to talk us out of it because he thought it would be useless. This outraged Karen and I. I then stated emphatically, "My life is at stake. I demand treatment that is bold, aggressive, decisive and rapid". I must have a PET scan and, if it shows the cancer has not spread, I must have liver surgery to remove the tumor". The oncologist stated that he would present my case before a meeting of the tumor board – a group of oncologists, surgeons, pathologists and research scientists – that was scheduled for later that week and that the results of this meeting would decide the course of my treatment.

Karen and I left the hospital in stunned silence. Neither of us spoke for almost a half hour until Karen received a call on her cellphone. This was a heavy blow, the most immediate mortal threat of my entire cancer journey. All we could do was wait for the decision of the tumor board.

A tumultuous new chapter had begun. The finding of a malignant tumor in my liver shattered the image - promoted by my doctors and eagerly shared by Karen and I - that I was a poster-child for pancreatic cancer treatment at Beth Israel Deaconess Medical Center. Moreover, the newly diagnosed cancer metastasis filled Karen and I with intense fear. The overall odds of surviving pancreatic cancer are about five percent. In contrast, after pancreatic cancer spreads to the liver or other tissues, the odds of survival drop drastically, to about one in several thousand. Karen and I were in disbelief. After my fabulous rebound from initial cancer treatment to vigorous good health and after a year living and working in a tropical paradise, was all lost? Was this IT?

Chapter 21

Fate Takes a Vacation

"Woke up this mornin'. Smiled at the risin' sun. Three little birds on my door step… singing sweet songs, melodies pure and true. This is my message to you: "Don't you worry about a thing, 'cause every little thing's gonna be all right", Bob Marley.

A few days later, on Wednesday afternoon, April 28th, we got the call from my oncologist. The tumor board had met and made their decision. A PET scan to assess the degree of cancer spread was scheduled for the following Tuesday, May 4. Karen and I were looking at each other with tears and apprehension when she suddenly produced a stroke of genius. "Let's go to St. Maarten for the weekend", she said. "We have to close your apartment anyway, you can explain things to your colleagues in person and you and I will have some fun and take our minds off the bad stuff". So, the very next morning, we took off for the island of impossibly good weather, great beach bars and perpetual Coppertone tans. During the flight down, Karen and I reviewed our lives, my health prospects and our plans going forward. It had to be the most emotion-packed hours we've ever spent together.

That Friday evening, a group of my St. Maarten medical school friends and colleagues treated Karen and I to a sumptuous outdoor dinner at our favorite French restaurant, Mati, at the edge of the Caribbean. Laughter and toasts of good heath and good wishes helped assuage our painful thoughts. The next morning they helped us pack and store the contents of our apartment. We then spent Saturday and Sunday afternoons at Baie Rouge, my favorite beach, a place were all one's troubles can melt away into the sand and surf. Imagine warm crystal clear blue-green water, as gentle as a bathtub and surrounded by cliffs with beautiful villas, shack restaurants right there with delicious grilled meats and salads and a live band playing Bob Marley's song and other mellow island tunes. "It's happy owwa, mon,...2 for 1". For most of that weekend, all fear of dreadful PET scan results, possible liver surgery and more chemotherapy completely subsided... my soul was soothed...for a while.

Fast-forward to PET scan day. Bob Marley wasn't with me that morning. I woke up without smiling at the sun or hearing the birds Bob sung about. I was just plain petrified. "What if I lit up all over me?", I thought, "God help me".

Amazingly, the PET scan results provided no evidence that the pancreatic cancer spread beyond my liver. Thankfully, this remarkable finding provided Karen and I with a much needed dose of new hope. Intense fear subsided and I was scheduled to meet with a liver surgeon, Dr. Douglas Hanto, at the Beth Israel Deaconess Liver Transplant Center.

Chapter 22

Chopped Liver, Another Brush with the Paranormal and a Hot Head

I was very fortunate that Dr. Hanto, a liver transplant surgeon was consulted as part of the tumor board that decided my course of treatment. Several years earlier, when Dr. Hanto was at another hospital, he had operated successfully on a patient whose pancreatic cancer had spread to his liver. This patient's tumor was contained in his liver, had not spread, and when the tumor was removed, he had returned to good health. Dr. Hanto was hopeful that my case would be similar. By comparison with a liver transplant operation, my surgery involved removal of only a piece of my liver, and since the tumor was only about an inch and a half long, the liver portion to be excised was not too large. Unlike the pancreas, which does not self-regenerate after surgery to remove part of it, liver tissue does regenerate. I was not a heavy drinker of alcohol and, aside from pancreatic cancer, generally in very good health. If removal of the tumor was successful, my liver function was expected to recover. Because of Dr. Hanto's busy surgical schedule, my operation was planned for 10 days later.

My colleagues at the medical school in St. Maarten were aware of my surgery schedule and soon after Karen said goodbye to me at the surgical preparation area, she received an email from the dean with the following message to all faculty and students: "Our beloved friend, colleague and faculty member, Dr. Steven Lewis, is scheduled for surgery today at Beth Israel Hospital in Boston. Steven has inspired many of us as a faculty member and pancreatic cancer survivor. He is authoring a book pertaining to his journey of healing and views the current episode as yet another chapter to write. To show support for Steven, his wife Karen and their family, we have scheduled a gathering today in the campus rotunda so we can stand together in a circle of healing". Later when Karen was waiting for me to emerge from surgery she received another email with the photo below. She was amazed at the coordinated timing between the Caribbean and Boston, let out a shriek of surprise and proudly showed the photo of the prayer vigil to the others in the waiting room.

The "circle of healing" assembled for me at the American University of the Caribbean School of Medicine, St. Maarten.

My liver surgery proceeded smoothly and successfully. There was only one tumor. Dr. Hanto entirely removed it with more than adequate normal tissue surrounding it. So unless there was microscopic spread of the cancer that was impossible to detect by eye during the surgery, there was - after all the intense mortal fear – the possibility for a real cure. Only time would tell. Pancreatic cancer normally spreads quite aggressively. Microscopic buds of tumor cells could rapidly appear elsewhere. Periodic CAT scans of my abdomen and chest, along with measures of my CA 19-9 blood marker of tumor growth would be needed for surveillance.

My recovery from liver surgery was rapid and I was released from the hospital only two days later. What a joy to be home again and potentially cured. I awoke in bed very early - about 4 AM – the next morning to another paranormal experience that, like the bolts of energy that had jolted me upright in the Berkshires, seemed to portend a very positive outcome. As soon as I awoke, I had the sensation that a channel about 3 inches wide had opened, like the sunroof of a car, from the front to the back of the top of my skull. Into this opening poured beams of positive energy in the form of white fluffy particles coming from the sky. I felt this energy pouring in for some time and filling my entire body. After a while, my body felt so full of these particles, that I felt any cancer cells would have no room to grow and no where to go. This very intense experience is unforgettable.

On the morning following this new paranormal episode, I again awoke early, this time to a quite different experience. My head and entire body was literally full of heat…my temperature had spiked to 105° Fahrenheit. I had a post-surgical check-up scheduled for that morning and tried to keep Karen from panicking with jokes about me being a "hot-head". She was not amused. Likely, a major infection was brewing. It was a very warm day and, as the infection stoked my fever, it was very tough just to walk from our car to Dr. Hanto's office. "You've got an infection we have to deal with", he said, as he prepared orders for my readmission to the hospital.

Chapter 23

Hitting Bottom and Rebounding

My hospitalization to battle this infection lasted more than three weeks. This was a very rough stretch for Karen and me, Dr. Hanto and the infectious disease specialists tried every antibiotic and nothing seemed to work. My fever persisted and I was horribly weak from the surgery and related loss of blood. Each day, Karen would visit the hospital, find me uncomfortable and semi-coherent and hold wet washcloths on my forehead. For her, my battle with the infection was worse than my cancer battle. When Dr. Hanto made rounds and entered my hospital room, Karen could readily sense his frustration with the limited punch of the antibiotics he was giving me. This caused her great concern for my life.

In spite of all precautions to insure untainted blood, I preferred not to have a transfusion. In addition to my low blood count and my high fevers that caused extreme fatigue, I suffered through numerous other miseries such as middle of night wake-ups for procedures needing CAT scan guidance to drain abdominal infection fluid, having my thorax punctured to drain fluids, numerous vein punctures in both hands and arms and associated aches and pains of a complex surgical recovery. Because of all this, there were times I literally thought I'd be better off in a trash bag hauled away in some dumpster.

During these rough times, the combined pounding of life-threatening illness, recovery from surgery and the misery of acute infection brought my body and spirit to the lowest point of my life. Everyone has his or her own "bottom" and, even if I wasn't at that absolute, I surely was close. It was there, in my dark, foreboding "spiritual basement" that I came face to face with stark realities of persistence through life's difficulties.

After some time in this deeply depressed state, the bubble wrap of self-protective emotions that had brought me to that moment in life had been entirely stripped away and I reached a point of clarity. The mental process I had undergone was like unraveling a patchwork quilt made up of feelings of life-long accrued successes, failures, hurts, disappointments, unachieved goals, unresolved conflicts and compensatory ego-boosts. At that point of clarity during which I came face to face with my inner self, I had reached the core of my soul, the virtual ground zero of my being. And, to my amazement, the great thing was that I found it was not such a terrible place to be. I realized then I was basically a contented person and that I could and would get through this. I knew that from here upward was the only way I could go and I gathered all my resolve to move in that direction. During those moments, in a flash of insight, I internalized true empathy for the plight of others. As physically tormented as I was, I realized that many people in this world have suffered much more. So there was no excuse to feel sorry for myself. I reluctantly accepted a blood transfusion and the doctors finally gave me massive doses of the strongest infection-fighting antibiotics. This, plus my experience with two-a-day high school football practice in blistering heat and sweltering humidity eventually helped me persevere. As Nat King Cole said, "Pick yourself up, dust yourself off and start all over again".

Karen also hit her "spiritual basement" during the weeks I was hospitalized with the infection. Late one night, after she had been with me all day during one of my worst days, Karen reached exhaustion and did not know if she could continue watching me delusional and in misery. She whispered, "I'll see you in the morning" and left. When Karen got home, she sat on the bed fully dressed wondering what was happening to her husband. She put her head on the pillow and the next thing she knew it was morning. As the sun came in the window, Karen arose, removed her clothes and make-up from the day before, took a shower, got dressed, jumped in the car and drove to the hospital. She was frightened and did not know what to expect. The thought crossed her mind that she might walk into my room and find me gone. For Karen, these were the scariest moments of the entire cancer journey.

It already was late morning when Karen got off the elevator on the floor of my hospital room. She rounded the nurse's station at great speed and sprinted to my room. "Please let him be there" was all Karen kept thinking. She opened the door and there I was, sitting up in bed and saying matter-of-factly, "Why are you so late"? Very late the night before, the antibiotics finally started winning the battle and my fever broke. I was back and smiling again!

The intensity of my infection experience was enormous but not without positive by-products. During this time, I learned profound lessons of empathy and humility. Even though I was the person whose life had been threatened by metastatic pancreatic cancer and was suffering through a miserable infection, I even began to feel sorry for Dr. Heffernan's discomfort with telling me I likely had fatal cancer because he was not used to breaking such bad news.

Chapter 24

Don't Let Go of the Little Kid

There is a little kid that exists within me, a perpetual youngster that has salient characteristics vital to my ability to deal with recurrence of pancreatic cancer and vanquish a stubborn, severe infection. The little kid in me is between about 4 and 8 years old; old enough to look with wide-eyed wonder at the simplest things in life and to laugh in situations adults often take so seriously.

Me at about 6 years old...

The little kid is like a mental alter ego, tethered to my brain by a high-speed wireless interface. However, in my mind's eye, this virtual connection is "hard-wired". As life is lived at its various paces, I can imagine an actual physical connection or bridge to my little kid. I could be holding my kid's hand as he and I stroll or skip off together. He might be sitting in the basket of my bicycle as I cruise around the neighborhood. Or, when living life in a faster lane, my little kid could be securely strapped in the sidecar of a Harley.

When I was seriously ill, the little kid was a remarkable companion. In his kid's mind, the hospital is a just a place where you go for a while to get better, and then you come home and play again. To the little kid, people don't stay in the hospital very long and there is no knowledge of complications or things getting worse. If I look or feel really bad, it might completely escape the little kid, who is not used to noticing these things or at least may not directly connect them with an illness.

The little kid is completely uninhibited. While me, the grown-up hospital patient, grimaced at the next I.V. and tried to stay composed when the nurses didn't show up after repeated calls to minimize my discomfort, the little kid in me simply screamed, "Get me out of here!". Of course, the bellowing little kid was heard only by me, but his shrieks gave voice to my pain, and for that I am forever grateful!!

Without the little kid, the reality of time passing and its finite nature, would be more harsh, more brutal. When "grown-up time" becomes limited, fear and anxiety can overtake us. Deadlines, an impossibly crowded schedule or, more grimly, life-ending disease set us up for tough decisions requiring rapid action. Decisions made in apprehension and haste typically are flawed, leaving a string of unintended consequences that can wound loved-ones, friends and co-workers. The little tyke within me, however, is still too young to play basketball, so he or she has never been much interested in the "fast break". Instead, the little kid has all the time in the world. If the game he or she is engrossed in can't be finished right now, the little kid, if so inclined, can wait till after lunch. (For younger people reading this, I should point out that my own personal little kid exists an era prior to suburbs, soccer-moms and scheduled play times).

When hospitalized during the toughest times of my infection I clung tightly to the little kid as my physical and spiritual systems began to crash. Near my bottom, the thousand piece card table-sized jigsaw puzzle that - figuratively speaking - constituted my physical and spiritual health not only separated into each constituent piece, but scattered to every nook and cranny of the 10th floor liver transplant ward that housed my hospital room. The effort required to find each piece was excruciating, but equally enormous is the energy of a little kid. So "off the kid went" in boundless eagerness, as if searching for 1,000 afikomen at a Passover seder.

In the meantime, as I sat and pondered the extremely uncomfortable physical and mental sensations that dominated my physical and spiritual "basement", I could feel the little kid tugging at me, pulling on my hospital Johnny. As I sulked, the little kid was relentless. "Let's get out of here", he persisted. "There's lots of fun stuff we can be doing, but you got to be healthy and get out of this hospital".

The honest truth is that the urging of my mental alter-ego - a 4 to 8 year old kid that exists in my mind's eye - was vital to my battle upward from the physical and mental despair of severe acute infection. Moreover, the constant presence of my "little kid" is integral to what kept me moving forward in the face of life-threatening illness. With my "little kid" inside, I derive youthfulness, vitality and - if not the "immortality" of many 25 year olds - a vision of robust health for many, many years to come.

So, if you are like me, i.e. aware of an energetic "little kid" that lives within you, my advice is to not to forget or let go of the tyke. Instead, cultivate the relationship between you two. This bond can be extremely valuable when facing life's hardest challenges such as life-threatening disease, major accidents, divorce or the effects of environmental disasters.

Chapter 25

Over the Rainbow

It took more than three weeks for my infection to subside enough to permit my release from the hospital. My return home was not at all simple. For the time being, three tubes had to remain in my body. Two were drains stuck in my abdominal cavity to remove infection fluid that still accumulated. Another tube was placed in the large vein near my heart to facilitate continued delivery of intravenous antibiotics. My home care nurses and I were a team. They periodically checked and cleaned the openings around my tubes. I was in charge of daily collection and measurement of the quantity of fluid draining from my abdomen. A gradual reduction and stoppage of fluid drainage with passing time would indicate a decline in the extent of the infection. Other of my daily chores included injecting myself with intravenous antibiotics and also giving myself shots of blood clot dissolving medicine under the skin of my abdomen. A rigid schedule and careful procedures were needed and record keeping was important. I was a very busy guy!

As my home care proceeded, I visited Dr. Hanto's office for repeated check-ups and progress was slowly made. It was kind of like Dorothy's escape from Oz. My "Kansas" of good health finally seemed just over yonder. As time passed, infection fluid drainage eased and one of my two abdominal drains was removed. I was no longer the "Wizard of Ooze". The wicked witch was dead and the bluebirds were flying.

Like hurricanes, infection storms come and go. Mine was gradually reclassified from a Category 5 to a squall. With my temperature around normal and with my remaining infection fluid headed toward desiccation, I was feeling better each day and my doctors were ecstatic.

Karen's mood brightened and she began to marvel at my progress fighting the infection bug. As for me, I was amazed that my CA 19-9 blood tumor marker score - which was low-normal right after my liver surgery – continued to hover in that range. I hoped and prayed this score would stay low and urged my friends to do the same.

Karen and I were anxious to finally put this infection behind us as I beat back the last of the flying monkeys and continued down the yellow brick road toward good health. Chemotherapy had been planned to deal with potential microscopic cancer cells that persisted after my liver surgery. However, the time window during which chemotherapy would be of value was closing as the time needed to fight the infection increased. Also, my body's immune system could not handle both infection fighting and chemotherapy simultaneously. These conflicting issues added a new aspect of concern going forward. The tin man, scarecrow and lion were correct. It was definitely taking heart, brain and courage to traverse the road back to good health.

I tried very hard not to worry about chemotherapy or the lack of it. It was simply great to be recovering from the infection. I was getting ready to click my heels together three times... there was no place like home and feeling healthier.

Chapter 26

Chemotherapy and the Spirit in the Sky.

As recovery from my infection neared conclusion, I found myself in moments of deep contemplation over chemotherapy. Was my infection that delayed and likely prevented chemotherapy treatments itself an indirect "kiss of death"? Would chemotherapy even be necessary to kill remaining cancer cells or might it be harmful because it would weaken my immune system?

In one such moment of uncertainty, I said to myself, "Dear God". Immediately, I heard a deep resonant voice within me respond, "Are you addressing me"? "Yes, sir", I replied and God, like an Army drill sergeant, bellowed, "Don't call me *sir*. I have a title, my title is God and you will refer to me as such. "Do it again", snapped God, "and you go down for 25". Down for 25", I repeated to myself, "In the Army, that means 25 pushups". "Not so bad", I thought, "but there's no way that will happen in my post-surgical, recovering from infection mode". "But hey, I'm dealing with the Almighty here", I continued, trying as much as humanly possible not offend the Big Guy. "Who knows exactly what's up his sleeve"? So, unsure of exactly what He meant by "going down", or "for 25", I quickly whimpered, "Yes, I always will remember to address you as God".

"God", I continued, "my pancreatic cancer is a source of deep anxiety. I seem to be cancer free right now but chemotherapy might be needed to root out and slay any lingering cancer cells. The chemotherapy agents for pancreatic cancer are imperfect; their specificity and killing potential for certain types of pancreatic cancer are questionable. I've also been battling an infection and now chemotherapy may even be harmful. My oncologists tell me we won't know if I'm actually cured until 5 years have passed and I am still cancer free. To me, a black and white, "Got to see it in print" guy, all this is much too vague and I'm really apprehensive. As a young man, I was so darn healthy. I never dreamed the disease that had taken my mother also was in my future. Pancreatic cancer was just something I'd never signed up for".

For a long moment, God was quiet. Then, in a business-like but still sonorous tone He responded, "Of course, you yourself never signed up for this, what mortal would? It was, however, long ago inscribed in your book of life. I, as Master of the Universe, assure you that records of all aspects of your illness are documented in my Universal Master Plan and sealed for confidentially purposes in my own special "cloud computing" system. "May I get a copy?" I quickly blurted. "After all, according to HIPAA regulations, I am entitled access to my own health records". In response to this, God remained silent and I could sense His patience with me was wearing thin. "OK, sorry God, I muttered, I don't mean to burden you and your staff with Xeroxing chores. Maybe you can just give me the correct URL and I'll retrieve the record myself"? Completing this request, I sensed I had mistakenly treaded on sacred turf. At that instant, I saw God in my mind's eye, rolling His eyes and scowling. "My special cloud computing system is not Internet accessible", he roared. "That means no downloading, printing, copying or e-mailing to a friend". "But God, I meekly countered, "I'm a little scared. All I really want to know are your plans for my health over the next 5 years. Will I be cured, or will I by terrorized by another cancer outbreak"? At that, God's ire peaked and He snarled, "I don't allow mortals to see the future. You want predictions, try Nostradamus".

I remained silent, some moments passed and God seemed to regain His composure. "Look", he said more gently as if imparting a piece of His infinite wisdom, "you're no different from the rest of the world. All you mortals struggle and must carry on in the face of considerable doubt. After 9/11 your lives changed, adding many more hassles and uncertainties. You asked your presidents, "How will be know when the war on terrorism is over? "The end of the war will not be obvious", they replied. "There will be no direct surrender by the terrorists and no peace treaties signed. "Instead, when terrorist acts such as hijackings and bombings cease, we will realize that hostilities are over". "Such is your pancreatic cancer." God thoughtfully continued. "After the tumor was discovered in your pancreas, the lives of you, your wife and your other family members changed drastically, often stressing all of you out and leaving you with deep concerns for the future. Things were quiet for 3 years but then, analogous to a terrorist "sleeper cell", some of the pancreatic cancer cells that had escaped detection migrated to your liver, recruited more members and launched the attack you are presently recovering from. At this juncture, you'll have to endure 5 more years of extreme vigilance, repeated surveillance by MRIs, CATscans and PETscans to assess the level of cancer cell "chatter" indicating or threatening disease. Like victory over terrorism, the end of your war with pancreatic cancer also will not be obvious". "You won't hear the fat lady sing or see the goalposts demolished", He added in a father-like manner. "Instead, it will be a private special moment you and your family will cherish, celebrate and forever hold sacred". "But remember", God concluded, "I'm not making any promises".

Chapter 27

A New Tumor?

A few weeks after the drains used to remove infection fluid from my abdomen were finally pulled, I began to notice a bulge under the skin over the area of my liver that was gradually increasing in size. "Oh my God, what is that? Could that be another tumor?", said a distressed Karen. Nervously, I made an appointment with my liver surgeon Dr. Hanto whose care I was still under until my post-surgical infection completely disappeared. As I walked from the parking lot to Dr. Hanto's office, down Brookline Avenue, a major thoroughfare near the cluster of Boston hospitals that include Beth Israel Deaconess Medical Center, Brigham and Women's Hospital, Dana Farber Cancer Center and Children's Medical Center, I spotted a familiar face in the distance and started to wave. It was Dr. Mark Callery, the always warm and engaging surgeon who had performed my Whipple operation more than three years earlier. I knew Dr. Callery was aware of my liver metastasis because he had visited me briefly when I was hospitalized with my major infection. "Hi Dr. Callery, nice to see you", I said. "I've been feeling much better and my infection is almost gone, but something has been growing under the skin near my liver and I'm on my way to see Dr Hanto about it right now". Without hesitation in the middle of all the passers-by, Dr. Callery said, "Let me have a look". So I opened my jacket, lifted my shirt and received a quick examination by a renowned surgeon in the middle of a busy Boston street. "What is it? Does it look like a tumor", I asked. "I'm not sure, but it could be", Dr.

Callery replied, "and it needs to be taken care of quickly". With this in mind, my apprehension grew as I continued toward Dr. Hanto's office.

"Dr. Hanto", I said as he examined me, "I have to tell you that, fortuitously, I just received a "second opinion" on this problem on Brookline Avenue while walking to your office". I proceeded to relate my chance meeting with Dr. Callery. Dr. Hanto then explained that the bulge in my skin might be a cancerous growth resulting from a "tumor ladder". This could occur if cancer cells remaining from my liver surgery migrated up the drains that were in my abdomen, lodged under my skin and began to multiply. He would have to remove the growth and, in order to know for sure what caused it, send a sample to pathology for tests. He then scheduled me for yet another surgery at Beth Israel Deaconess Medical Center.

The plan was for a short surgery that had me under general anesthesia for about one hour. As this point, Karen and I were numb. We already had been through just about everything and knew it was best to remain agitation free. On the morning I checked in for surgery, my infection was practically gone and I was feeling good physically and generally upbeat. The doctor assigned to insert my I.V. gave up after two or three tries. She was very apologetic and I tried to console her by saying I'd been through much worse. She and the surgical nurse that finally inserted my I.V. began to ask me the standard questions asked of all patients at Beth Israel. "Can you please rate your pain on a scale from 0 to 10"?. "Zero", I answered, because I was not feeling pain. "Do you feel safe in your relationships"? I hesitated for an instant and then answered, "Yes, but not with my mortgage company or the IRS". After they cracked up with laughter, they sedated me and the next thing I knew, I awoke and saw Dr. Hanto above me. "Everything is fine", he said. "There were no tumor cells, only infection material".

I had dodged yet another bullet. The fact that Dr. Hanto very aggressively removed a much larger area than the bulge in my skin did not bother me. In case there was a tumor, he had to excise normal tissue in order to be sure he got it all. The half egg-sized crater in the skin over my abdomen became just another battle scar like those from my Whipple and liver operations.

Chapter 28

Stop and Think! Increasing Your Thread Count in the Texture of Life

"It's my body, it's my life and it's my future",
Mindy Lewis, at 5 years old.

Two weeks after my Whipple surgery, I received a birthday card that said in big bold letters, "STOP AND THINK". I saved this card and would look at it many times during my cancer journey… it influenced me to regularly stop and think about life. A cancer journey is not simply a battle to restore physical health. There also are tremendous emotional forces at work. While my life was "on hold" during the long period of treatment and recuperation, there was ample time to reexamine relationships with family, relatives and friends and to consider life before, during and after cancer. This was an opportunity to grow emotionally and part of my mission as cancer patient was to turn my sickness inside out, learn from it and maximize all its positive aspects.

My time of treatment and recovery from life-threatening illness therefore was a time to take stock of "my body, my life and my future." I finally admitted I am not immortal and, going forward, my life, health and family are top priority. Before my cancer journey, I was "too busy" with other things and did not spend a lot of time clearly reflecting on life. In reality, when people are "too busy" to do some specific thing, they are making the choice that the thing they are too busy to do really is not their top priority. For me, stopping and thinking meant "turning inward" to focus time and energy on health, feelings about going through my cancer journey and family. I focused on the "care and feeding of me" and each second became precious. To paraphrase the country song of Tim McGraw, whose father, former NY Mets pitcher Tug McGraw died of brain cancer, it became clear to me that I needed to "...live each day as if I were dying".

Reflection during my time of "stopping and thinking" gave me much more "life texture", i.e. a better understanding of why my life is a certain way and how the events of my life were woven together. One way to envision life texture is to view it as analogous to the thread count of cotton. This metaphor clarified itself to me when, on a shopping trip for pillowcases, I took the opportunity to "*shop* and think". During my pillowcase quest, I learned that both the basic quality of the cotton and the fabric thread count both determine the feeling of comfort. We each are born with - and in our early development achieve - certain basic qualities, like the quality of cotton. Our experiences as we proceed through the rest of our lives contribute - like the thread count of cotton - to the texture of our lives. No one's life is perfect...every one of us has both major and minor obstacles to overcome. Regularly stopping and thinking is a practice that can add important texture, and therefore comfort, to our lives. Regular reflection can help us deal more effectively with the many layers of life's complexities and help us to better understand how to smooth them out. This is a very useful practice for those on a cancer journey and anyone else passing through major life difficulties.

One way I increased my life texture was by adding spirituality as an important new dimension to my life. My paranormal experiences with the force fields that jolted me upright after my cancer diagnosis and with the positive energy that beamed down into me from the sky after my liver surgery were key elements in my acceptance of spiritually. *As a scientist* for most of my adult life, I had the attitude that *all must be provable* to be considered real. From my scientific side, real healing in my body would be based on objective evidence that my cancer was gone. However, after my paranormal experiences, the *spiritualist* that now also resided within me resonated with the outlook that *not all needs to be proven, there is much that can just be felt.* Even though the spiritualist within me did not have the blessing of the scientist within me that my paranormal experience could or would lead me back to good health, my spiritual side definitely *believed* it. To my spiritualist alter ego, "feeling is healing". In contrast, my scientist alter-ego would say, "These paranormal experiences *probably* were nonsense" but just maybe… Including the words "*probably*" and "*just maybe*" signified my increase in life texture. Before I added my spiritual dimension, "my scientist" did not allow room for "my spiritualist". The increase in my life texture emanating from my new spirituality added gray to my scientific black and white. My spirituality signified a softening of the fabric of my life, and as I became more flexible, it allowed mental room for both my scientific and spiritual sides. I had thus found a new way of going forth.

Going through the process of stopping and thinking also has made me look toward old age as a period when, in spite of the likelihood of more aches, pains and illnesses, there also is time to construct a richer life texture…because there is more time to stop and think and to reflect on the many remarkably good things that life has brought. I hoped that my successful bout with cancer would someday let me reach old age when I can renew and expand the positive aspects of the reflection time I've recently had.

A major hurdle to be overcome when dealing with life-threatening illnesses such as these is "acceptance". One must come to terms with the illness and its potential consequences and accept rather than deny reality. This does <u>not</u> mean one should not fight as hard as possible to remain extremely positive and find the best doctors and treatments. It simply means that it is important to "stop and think" and pay close attention to what the illness and its attendant effects have in store for you and your family.

Chapter 29

Stop and Thank! Living With Uncertainty

> *"What a journey this has been. I've learned so much about life...going through all this with grace and a positive attitude has opened up a whole new world for me. I am grateful for this experience and what it has taught me."* Steven Lewis, CaringBridge.org journal entry, January 5, 2008.

After my treatments were complete, I was told I would need screening for tumor activity in the form of CAT scans or MRIs and CA19-9 tests at least every six months for several years. The realization that after treatment, I will have to live for a while with uncertainty about my health, was initially very anxiety provoking. However, after pondering this – and talking with friends who've had serious health issues or accidents – I came face to face with some key truths about life: 1) at some point we all will die, 2) *at any moment* any of us can die due to illness or accident, 3) we all live with constant uncertainty about our health and the health of our family members. No one truly knows what the future holds for his or her health or whether they will be in a serious accident. However, if you've had a serious illness or accident, you become much more aware of these realities. If you can, as mentioned above, "put it out to the Universe", you will better understand and accept that there are certain situations beyond your control and to some extent or other, you may have to deal with these situations as part of "going with the flow" of life.

Our genetics and accidents are largely out of our control. Lifestyle is something within our control and, depending on the extent of our genetic predisposition to one disease or another, lifestyle may modify our chance of suffering a particular disease. As the father of one of my friends used to say, "If you want to make sure you stay safe (from accidents), remain in bed all day." Unfortunately, remaining in bed all day is one way to increase your chances of developing a variety of chronic diseases relating to physical inactivity.

Habitual smoking increases the risk of pancreatic cancer. Other factors that may increase pancreatic cancer risk are obesity, a high meat, high fat diet and physical inactivity. I never smoked, was not obese, ate a reasonably good diet and was very physically active throughout life. My one risk factor was heredity...my mother died of pancreatic cancer. My cancer therefore, was essentially out of my control and, because of this, after my cancer diagnosis, I acquired the mindset that having a good attitude in dealing with my illness is the only logical choice. Having a good attitude holds no guarantee of being cured but it is more likely to provide you and your loved ones a better quality of life than pessimism in the face of disease.

The unfortunate truth for all of us is not *if* you or someone in your immediate family will be become seriously ill but *when* they will become seriously ill. No one - including me - wants to think serious illness can happen to us, but if you think honestly about it, at some point in life, it will happen to nearly all of us.

Because of the unpleasant nature of these thoughts, we avoid dwelling on illness and death, the fact that we could die at any moment and that fact that our health and that of our family members truly is uncertain. In large measure, avoidance of these issues helps us – on a day-to-day basis - lead productive and mentally healthy lives. Obsession with death and illness is, of course, highly dysfunctional. What many of us lack, however, is simply an occasional appreciation of the reality of sickness and mortality. Such an "occasional appreciation", arguably is an important feature of one's spirituality. And it is this aspect of our spirituality - momentarily stopping and being thankful for our current good health - that if put into practice, can help us navigate many of life's distressful events.

I think of it this way: I was diagnosed with pancreatic cancer, which has the highest mortality percentage of any cancer. There is no complete guarantee my treatments did cure me or will cure me of this disease. Because of this, there is uncertainty about my own premature mortality and whether I'll need to undergo additional treatments with extremely unpleasant side effects. What gets me through is my realization that everyone's life and health are in fact, precarious, and my determination to enjoy each moment, whether it is my last or one of many, many more in the long life I envision for myself.

Truthfully, I could never have had this perspective without experiencing life-threatening illness. I wish it didn't take peril to my life to reach this vantage point but do realize that none of us are eager to stop and consider our own mortality or that of our loved ones. Nevertheless, imagine that tomorrow you or one of your family is challenged by life-threatening disease. If you can put yourself into that scenario and try to understand what it really feels like, the terms "smell the roses" and "seize the day" take on a whole new meaning.

Chapter 30

Some Tips and Suggestions

> "Now I fully understand what was meant when my mother used to say, "You should live and be well". Steven Lewis, CaringBridge.org journal entry, January 1, 2008.

> "A large part of the nurturing I received from Karen emphasized laughter. We tried to make the best out of each situation by laughing and cracking outrageous jokes. Many of my humorous journal entries and many of your funny guest messages reinforced the positive spirit that helped carry me through. They say that laughter is the best medicine and I truly do believe it!!!", Steven Lewis, CaringBridge.org journal entry, June 19, 2008.

Even though this was not intended to be a self-help book, I thought it appropriate to share some useful tips and suggestions from the experience of my own cancer journey. Because each individual's illness and life situation is likely to be somewhat different, my suggestions are unlikely to be applicable to all. Several of these concepts have been mentioned earlier in this book but in the present chapter they are specifically called out and highlighted.

Key Points:

Open up to others about your illness and "accentuate the positive".
If you radiate positive energy, you will touch the lives of many
others in a positive way and you'll get back even more positive
energy than you give out. The positive energy you get back can
maximize your quality of life while you battle life-threatening
illness. On the other hand, complaining and being negative
and pessimistic is very likely to detract from the quality of life
for you and your loved ones.

*Be as flexible as you can in adapting yourself to the effects of
surgery, radiation, chemotherapy and medications.* These effects
will change over time as your body adjusts itself during
the various stages of your illness. So be prepared for many
changes in your body and try to "go with the flow" rather than
fight. You'll need all your energy to get well. Trying to resist
inevitable change will sap this energy.

Getting well after cancer is complex. It involves recovery from
different treatments - surgery, radiation and chemotherapy -
and the effects of the various medications you are taking. What
you are feeling on any given day is likely to change over time.
There are ups and downs you will experience and the task is to
get through minimal complaint, i.e. with a positive attitude.

Serious illness can be an opportunity for spiritual uplift. Try to
live as normal a life as you can. With any extra time you have,
do things you enjoy and also those you didn't do before you
were sick because you were too busy. If you can manage to
live a fairly normal life and also do things you were unable
to do when you were healthy, you'll feel less like your illness

has robbed you of life and more like you've grown from the experience.

Try to have a normal social life. If you can stay positive, you'll be amazed how supportive your friends can be. People can be greatly inspired to see you upbeat and graceful during tough times. They will return inspiration to you to endure and conquer your illness. For most of us, having a normal social life means meeting new people. If you stay positive when meeting new people and open up to them about your illness, you may be able to "recruit" them to join your healing team. Also, don't be afraid to go to reunions and be open about your cancer with old friends. You'll find many of them have battled cancer or other very serious illnesses. Their stories will inspire you, you will inspire them and you'll renew and richen old friendships.

Don't give up hope. Today, a small but growing number of patients with cancers once considered fatal are now being treated as individuals with chronic diseases ("Cancer as a disease, not a death sentence", J. Brody, New York Times, June 17, 2008). A plethora of new research findings are rapidly improving the prognosis for many cancers. Doctors, patients and their families are being given new hope. In increasing numbers, patients with once lethal cancers are kept alive by a succession of new treatments and in some cases eventually cured. Cancer in general and pancreatic cancer in particular is a fast-moving, explosive field. There many new discoveries that individual cancer doctors may not be aware of. For this reason, a second opinion may often be helpful.

Shortly after I completed chemotherapy, a friend of mine was diagnosed with advanced pancreatic cancer that had already spread to other organs. He believed he had only months to live and seemed like his hope was gone. When I saw him again only a few weeks later, he was still quite ill but looked much more robust and acted more hopeful. He was under the care of a doctor who, using new combinations of different chemotherapy drugs, had been keeping patients with advanced pancreatic cancers alive for as long as 5 to 6 years. Even though this new approach could not guarantee a cure, it was a way for my friend to buy time and create hope for a possible future cure.

You are definitely not alone. If you are diagnosed with cancer, you'll likely pay more attention than ever before to news reports about cancer discoveries and treatments, to stories of how cancer has touched friends and acquaintances, and to cases of celebrities stricken with cancer. What you'll find is that cancer is all around you. Rather than feel engulfed by cancer, a more positive approach is to realize there are plenty of people ready to share their experience and empathize with you. A support group of patients or former patients with similar types of cancers may complement the support of your caregiver, relatives and friends. If you feel a cancer patient support group may be helpful, my suggestion is to discuss this with a social worker or other professional counselor. Your counselor should be able to direct you to a support group where you best fit in.

In my case, I decided, rather than attend a traditional cancer support group, I would mostly derive support through my CaringBridge.org website and via visits and phone calls to friends and relatives. Pancreatic cancer is not common but when it occurs it is often deadly within several months. This was probably why I could not find a pancreatic cancer support group to attend. I did not want to attend a support group for patients with various cancers. I felt I could keep my own very positive attitude and would, if anything, get depressed by others' woes. For similar reasons, Karen also considered but did not join a support group for caretakers whose loved ones had a variety of different cancers.

Be selective in what you read; look for current, accurate information. My experience stresses the benefits of fostering and maintaining a positive attitude during a cancer journey. For this reason, I felt comfortable with my doctors' recommendations to largely avoid reading cancer *stories* on the web. Many of these stories do not have positive outcomes. If you dwell on them, these stories can be extremely depressing and can turn you negative and pessimistic. This happened to Karen when she Googled pancreatic cancer. Also, many web-published stories may not apply to you because it often is impossible to determine if stated side effects, treatment complications and negative outcomes were due to older methods, less experienced doctors and hospitals or patients with a variety of complicating medical conditions. There is, on the other hand, helpful new and accurate *information* about different types of cancers published on the Internet at sites such as Web MD, the Mayo Clinic website and the Johns Hopkins Medical School website.

I also did several extensive searches on Amazon.com for various types of cancer books. A problem is that cancer books may be out of date even if published just a few years ago. As I've mentioned, much of cancer treatment is changing and improving ("The new ways we fight cancer", S. Waxman and R. Gambino, Wall Street Journal, October 17, 2007). There is more hope all the time for less suffering during treatment and a better outcome. With newer and more specific treatments, side effects have been reduced and survival odds may be improved.

Epilogue

Today, May 20, 2014 marks exactly 4 years since my liver surgery to remove the pancreatic tumor that had metastasized to my liver. During all this time, my doctors have not detected any sign of cancer in my body. I have been in excellent health, eating right and exercising regularly. It all truly is a miracle!

Karen and I have relocated from Boston to Delray Beach, Florida. On long walks with our dogs each day, we take time to smell the roses. We often STOP AND THINK about the experiences described in this book, what we learned from our journey and we stop and give thanks for all the positive aspects of our lives.

I have joined Facebook groups focused on pancreatic cancer and surviving Whipple surgery. Even though several years have passed since I have been ill, I find participating in these groups can be informative and personally therapeutic. When appropriate, I offer what I feel may be helpful information or advice.

Presently, we have several relatives and friends on their own cancer journeys. We hope reading this book will help them and any of you on similar journeys through life's extreme difficulties.

Remember to keep a positive attitude and a smile on your face. This will ripple out to those around you and help you develop and maintain a community of caring individuals to support you.

Struggling to turn my attitude from negative to positive soon after my pancreatic cancer diagnosis and maintaining a positive attitude helped my family and me avoid severe emotional turmoil. Of course, it is beyond words that I survived this dreadful disease. But regardless of whether I survived or not, it is terrible to contemplate what an attitude of complaint and negativity would have done to my family and me. It was my own personal choice to become and remain positive…what would you have chosen to do?

Appendix

Quotes from CaringBridge.org: How Others Were Inspired by My Journey

<u>Peter W</u>: "We have become accustomed to sharing joyous times with you and Karen and seeing you both dodge life's bullets with aplomb. The kind of positive energy we have witnessed when your family gathers, rallies and deals with life's challenges, be it war in the Middle East or handling family interactions in this chaotic world are admirable. You guys, in a slow but sure way, seem to chew it up and spit it out. Your intellect, your family's flair for fun and community, and your collective energy are always impressive and exemplary. I am happy to burden you with further expectations! I know if anyone can rebound it is you, my friend. I know this journey is filled with fear, sadness and determination. But the love and support that surround you are what make the fight worthwhile. How paradoxically lucky you are! I hope every day becomes a healing one. My wishes are for you to gain the strength and a sense of real triumph as each day passes. I believe that this illness and the barriers it creates in your life will be short and temporary. You WILL win... i feel it... I know it. "GO FOR IT", Steven!"

<u>Nancy K.</u>: The CaringBridge.org website with the ability of guests to read each other's entries, really does lead to a community of caring."

<u>Howard and Florence</u>: "You're brave and open sharing this, thru CaringBridge…will bring many prayers from your friends and relatives across the country. The more prayers, the better."

<u>Hy R</u>: "…the love that flows on these pages will still be warming us when February's frost comes. Reading your updates and all the good wishes radiates like sunshine—and makes one stop to realize what's really important in our lives. Thanks for sharing this loving, very unique experience."

<u>Phil T</u>: "We have heard of your profound and challenging journey as experienced by those around you. Listening to their descriptions, and your words on this wonderful site, it would be impossible not to feel the love and compassion that has swelled between you and that has lifted you to such a clear and connected place from which to embrace life and to heal."

<u>Helen B</u>: "Every time we read your journal you are thanking all of us for our inspiration and support…but, hey…thank YOU, my friend. It is your strength, courage, determination and gratitude that have enriched all of us so much!"

<u>Michael K</u>: "Now that I have visited this site, your strength literally jumps out of the computer screen."

<u>Gail N</u>: "Seeing you on New Year's eve was a warm and wonderful treat! I am still feeling the love. I have already shared your story and this site with another friend in the Berkshires, who will share it with a friend of hers. So thank you on many levels from many people."

Steve A: "I for one, find that your stories really lift me up. Sorta like you're medicine for the rest of us."

Tamar A: "Your journey to recovery makes me realize that even if I'm down about anything, I should perk right up and enjoy the day and life in general, and that's a powerful and inspirational message! Keep doing what you're doing. You're not just bettering yourself, but you're making us all better in many ways."

Kathryn and Marc: "The journey is not one we would ask for, but it definitely teaches us much that we might have otherwise missed."

Gail N: "Glad all reports are positive. Your courage and enthusiasm is the best medicine, not only for you, but for all of your loving fans! Reading the well wishes of all of your friends and family with whom I share these pages…some whom I know and others who I feel like I know, tells me life is good and we are all better for having you in our lives."

Delight: "It's truly a privilege, Steve, to follow your fearful journey and see how you are managing it. It is great and such an inspiration."

Jennifer and Stacy: "Your courage and even humor during this ordeal of ordeals has been extraordinary. You are so right, and how good it is to be reminded, that each day we open our eyes and look forward to a productive, healthy day is a gift."

Acknowledgements

Without my "beautiful bride" and exceptionally loving caretaker, Karen Lewis, this book simply would not have been written. For 45 years, she has been with me every step of the way. It was at Karen's urging that I began work on this book and it was her emotional recall of many specific moments during my cancer journey that gave explicit narrative to my accurate recounting of key events. Karen persistently encouraged me to complete the book and she proof-read and provided valuable comments on each version. She has been my inspiration.

My son, Ryan Lewis, provided his exceptionally loving heart and U.S. Army "can do" attitude as reinforcements to Karen and I during my health battles. His determined spirit and enthusiastic willingness to do whatever was necessary were ever-present.

The love and support of my daughter and her husband, Mindy and Jon Zald, and my in-laws, Rhoda and David Gelber, is gratefully appreciated.

Many others contributed to the successful navigation of my cancer journey and completion of this book ...

A special thank you is reserved for Rena Wolner. Rena's valuable critique and experience in her distinguished career as a publishing executive spurred my final push to complete this project and inspired the book's title.

Laura Yorke and Gary Rosenberg also made important contributions to the development of this book.

All the people deserving of acknowledgement for their efforts and ideas during my cancer journey and preparation of this book are too numerous to mention. A special thanks goes to those who sent notes of encouragement to my CaringBridge. org webpage.

Of course, this book would not have been written without my outstanding team of doctors – Mark Callery, Douglas Hanto, Anand Mahedevan, Michael Goldstein, James Heffernan, Alphonso Brown and Talya Schwarzberg – at Beth Israel Deaconess Medical Center in Boston. They and the other Beth Israel Deaconess health care professional – including nurses, social workers, hospital attendants and administrative assistants – provided me with a standard of treatment that is difficult to match.

31522978R00091

Made in the USA
San Bernardino, CA
11 March 2016